Grace Grid:

A Theological Foundation

Grace Grid

By: Eric Matthew Johnson
5 Stones Publishing © 2013

For permission to translate contact the publisher.
Published By
5 Stones Publishing
2001 W. 6th Street E12
Lawrence, Kansas 66044
Email: randy2905@gmail.com
www.ilncenter.com
ISBN 978-1-935018-82-7

5 Stones Publishing is a division of the
International Localization Network
© 2013 All Rights Reserved

Interior Book Design R.E. Johnson
Cover designed by Brandon A. Johnson
The ILN Design Team

To my sister,

for showing me that words change things

Contents

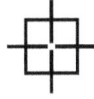

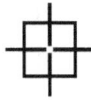

Foreword

Derek Levendusky

Hiroo Onoda was a Japanese soldier in World War II who was sent to Lubang Island in the Philippines on December 26, 1944, with simple orders to gather intelligence and defend the island against the Allied Forces. Though the war ended in 1945, he and three other soldiers fought for years in the jungles against what they thought were Allied Forces masquerading as local authorities and civilians. They killed and injured many people. Eventually, his three comrades died, and he was left alone for years, he believed, to continue his solemn duty to defend the island for his native Japan. On March 10, 1975, he finally surrendered, 29 years after the war had ended. Only then did he realize the war was, in fact, over.

For 29 years, Onoda fought and suffered for nothing. His comrades died for nothing. How often is this a picture of struggling Christians? They suffer unnecessarily because, like Onoda and his comrades, they don't know the truth that the war is over, that Jesus won the victory at the cross, and that God is sovereign.

The Bible says in Hosea 4:6, *"My people are destroyed for lack of knowledge."* Jesus said in John 8:32, *"You will know the truth, and the truth will set you free."*

Healthy doctrine precedes a healthy experience. Theology is not just for bookish people, Bible school students, and doctrinaire debaters. It's for our blessing and life! As Sinclair Ferguson put it in his book *The Christian Life,* "Knowing is for living!"

If you define theology as "the study of God," then by that definition, we're all theologians. The question is: Are you a good one or a bad one?

Meanwhile, the Scriptures lie waiting, like an invitation to a wedding, for us to come, hear, comprehend, believe, obey, and live. To ignore them, to assume the gospel, and to discard doctrinal precision as unnecessary or divisive is to err to our own hurt, if not our own destruction. As a pastor, I have seen that what seem to be minor errors in understanding the gospel early on results in big problems later.

Friend and author Eric Johnson gives us the opportunity in this powerful little book to attend the apostles' table and hear again, or perhaps for the first time, the precious and powerful doctrines on which we can build our lives.

Knowing this brother personally, I have often heard the passion in his voice and seen the zeal in his eyes as he discusses the gospel. Only a man who knows the power of it in his own soul can truly share the good news that it is. The work that is in your hands is not simply a thesis or a whimsical blog; to my friend, the doctrines herein have been life and power. I know that it's the great desire of his heart, not only to experience its joys himself, but also to offer them to others. In a day when so many books are written to sell to great audiences a watered-down, marketable, Christless Christianity, this time you can expect to read a book that presents the timeless, unshakable truths from a young man who loves Jesus and His church.

One of my teachers once told me that it is not the duty of today's preachers and teachers to say something new (God forbid!), but to say something true in a new way. Though the doctrines contained herein are not new, they are true, and, as they emerged from this pilgrim's journey with Christ, I believe we will find fresh fire in them.

I once believed the most important of all spiritual disciplines was prayer or Bible-reading, or perhaps fasting. As I've grown in understanding the gospel, I'm convinced that the most important discipline is *believing*. It is remaining in a place of faith in the finished work of Christ and His word. If our disciplines don't lead us to this place, they become dead works. Our spiritual disciplines ought to feed our faith in Jesus, who He is, and what He has done. As Tim Keller has said, "The gospel is not the ABCs of our faith, but the A to Z." We do not graduate from the gospel but only come into a deeper understanding of it. May this book add to that precious place in your life. May it strengthen your blessed instinct and practice of faith. May it inspire you to believe!

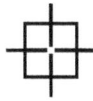

Introduction

My Journey

I entered Bible school in 2006. I was young, obviously, having just graduated from high school. I was naïve. I was not only naïve, I was home-schooled naïve. I had been raised in a Pentecostal Christian home and knew much of that culture. My dad had operated in the secular workplace, as well as every sort of ministry. He had worked in federal court. He had been a youth pastor and an associate pastor. Not only that, but my entire family spent a year and a half in Bosnia Herzegovina as missionaries. My small Bible college was born out of the Pentecostal tradition, so this allowed my life to continue in the course it had been headed thus far.

My rather diverse yet sheltered upbringing made for an interesting entrance into Bible college. I had a moderate interest in Scripture from the beginning. I had questions, and many of the more pressing ones were answered within my first year. Overall, I was encouraged in my rather conservative Pentecostal world view. I'm grateful for this to this day.

All that being said, there was one problem. Before I entered Bible college, I didn't have very much direction in my life. I had some vague dreams of film school. I had some inkling that God may have wanted me in the ministry. Because of this division in my mind, I was unable to get all that I could out of the first two years of the three I spent at this school. However, by my third year, something began to change. I began to see a need in the local church to which I never expected to give much thought. I began to see that in the local church, there were a great many people who had a zeal for God, but were surprisingly unfamiliar with His Word. I was unsure if this would eventually require any investment on my part.

After I graduated, I had begun to grow more curious if I might be one who would contribute to this need that I saw. I moved on to an accredited school in order to finish my undergraduate work. While I initially went with hopes of growing more passionate in my pursuit of theology, there were some authors that began to make me question the importance of doctrinal precision. It was at this time that I began to grow lax in my theological convictions. I began to feel at home in a place of uncertainty regarding the many questions that fascinated me. This lasted for several months.

There was one group of friends I had, however, that seemed to have gained a different set of priorities in the midst of this phase of their lives. The problem was, most of them were not Pentecostal. Most of them came from a more Reformed persuasion. It was around this time that I read a book by a Reformed author which called into question many of the authors that I had been so fascinated with in months gone by. It was at this point that I knew I needed to make a few changes in my thinking. I was by no means interested in letting go of my Pentecostal heritage, yet I knew that I would need to look elsewhere for theologians who would answer many of the nagging questions I was beginning to have.

I found myself caught between two worlds. I had a love for the gifts of the Spirit, yet at the same time I had a growing love for sound doctrine, particularly as I was finding it expressed by these Reformed theologians. This is where I found myself as I finished school.

After I received my undergraduate degree, I decided to take a semester off and help my dad with a project in Bosnia where I had spent time years before. It was there that I truly decided to dedicate myself to understanding the doctrines I had begun to explore and the way these friends of mine understood Salvation. I wanted to understand God's sovereign grace in the lives of His people. By the time I returned to America, I was torn in two. I had fallen in love with great preachers like Sam Storms and John Piper, yet I knew that much of their theology didn't fall into the Pentecostal categories that I had been so thoroughly raised in. I still had a love for the supernatural work of the Holy Spirit in the life of His church, yet I had a growing passion for God's sovereignty as it has been historically articulated in the Reformed tradition.

I had been overseas for two months when I finally returned home. It was then that I decided to read "The

Freedom of the Will" by the great 18th century preacher and theologian Jonathan Edwards. It was at this point that God's sovereignty and the doctrines of grace were solidified in my heart. The timing was perfect. It was at this point that I realized God had been moving in the lives of leaders that I knew. The foundational doctrines of the Reformed tradition were converging with much of the Charismatic tradition in their hearts as well. As I began to settle into my home town again, I got involved with a newly planted church where the tension in my theological world-view could be embraced in unity. I have been attending there ever since.

My Goal in This Work

The reason I tell my story in this way is because I know that many of my readers will be likely to also have a growing curiosity concerning many of the theological issues I have been hinting at. While many of you may not consider yourselves to be theologians, you may have begun to feel a certain measure of unrest in the amount of sound doctrine you have received over the years as you have attended church and have heard the word of God preached.

In this work, I have decided to lay out the basic doctrines and practices of the Christian faith as best I can. I plan to tackle the Christian understanding of Scripture, then a Scriptural view of God, creation, humanity, the gospel, the church, and the second coming of Christ. My readers will hopefully find an appreciation for both the worlds I have been describing. There is material that shows a belief in and a desire for the move of the Holy Spirit, yet the doctrines of salvation are deeply Reformed. Because I am aware that the doctrines of grace I am describing will likely be very new and difficult for many readers, I will be dedicating a good deal more space on this topic in chapter 6 than in the other chapters. I have found that while these doctrines are often bitter in the mouth, they are eternally sweet to the soul.

I truly hope that this work will help people to nail down a basic understanding of their faith. It is certainly not my goal to pursue every topic as far as I possibly can, but I hope that it will inspire whoever reads it to pursue the study of whatever topic captures his attention. To help in this pursuit, each chapter ends with one or more recommended books that address the issue just covered. I recommend that you read with an open Bible. There will be many verses and extended passages cited, many of which are not laid out on the page. I have chosen the ESV for the passages I do in fact quote.

As you read this book, I hope that it helps further you in your pursuit of knowing God.

~Eric J.

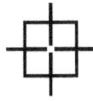

The Biblical Foundation

If anyone's will is to do God's will, he will
know whether the teaching is from God.
-John 7:17

Objective vs. Subjective

No matter who you are and no matter what side of the world you woke up on this morning, there are a few things that most likely did not happen as you got out of bed. It is likely that you didn't worry whether you would have trouble keeping yourself on the floor as you got dressed—as if you would suddenly float to the ceiling. You probably didn't worry about whether or not the numbers in your checkbook would continue to do their job, as if one plus one would suddenly equal three.

There are certain realities we take for granted in this life. We take them for granted to such an extent that we don't even begin to think about them unless we stop and make an intentional effort to bring them to our minds. This is the nature of objective reality. Unless someone is steeped in epistemological study (the study of how one gains knowledge), it isn't likely that he or she will regularly question the validity of the basic reality that each person experiences every day.

On the other hand, there are realities that we question on a daily basis. These realities exist in our emotions. They exist in our relationships. They exist in our ethics. They exist every time we need to make a painful choice. These are our subjective realities. While our objective reality is ever in the background, our subjective reality confronts us at every turn.

One aspect of reality that we take for granted is the fact that other minds exist in this world. We rely on this assumption every time we interact with another human being. This is where the subjective and the objective meet. It is here that we assume common ground. While the subjective reality of two human beings only exists in their own experience, they must assume that there is something outside of them both with which they can both find solidity. This is the only way that they can bring their subjective minds into a relational alignment. It is objective reality that determines whether two subjective minds can enjoy an experience together. It determines whether they can hate it, be indifferent to it, remember it, or simply forget it. These two ways of understanding reality are the basis for all life experience. It is true for individuals or multiple people in relationship to each other.

The Need for Something Solid

It is in the midst of this human experience, we have all, at one point or another, reached a dilemma. Human beings disagree. This ranges from the smallest areas of life to the most profound. At the core of our being, we know that there is objective reality. Deep down, we know that we all stand on some common ground. However, while we know we experience so many things in common, there are ways in which our thoughts, our opinions, and our perspectives refuse to line up.

This brings about the ultimate question. Is it possible for humanity to come to agreement on the nature of objective reality? This is what divides humanity and splinters it into all of its diversity. While there is great beauty in much of the diversity we see, we know that diversity has brought about everything from appreciation to violence.

All of this leads us to ask, what if it could be possible that the answer is yes? What if the truth can in fact be known? If it can, the ramifications of this become immediately obvious. This would mean that there are some who may have had the privilege of finding this truth. There may be some who have experienced it. This would also mean there are many who have not. If this is true, then it means there are some who need help from others to see reality for what it is. This would mean that some are right and some are wrong.

This is where we will begin. This is among the foundational values of the Christian faith. Christians believe in the reality of a knowable, objective truth. Not only that, we don't see that truth as an *it*, but as a *Him*. For the Christian, God is the starting point of all reality. While this entire introductory train of thought has focused on us, beginning with God forces the train of thought to begin again from *Him*.

If reality starts with God, it is His opinions that matter most. It is God who puts demands on the world and decides the way reality functions. It is His opinion that we should seek above all things. This leads to the next foundational belief of the Christian faith.

God Speaks

Another defining aspect of Christianity is the belief that this God is fully capable of communicating. It is our belief that this is the true origin of all we affirm about the supernatural. The Christian faith didn't come from the minds of human beings, but from the mind of God. He brought reality into being and therefore He can speak into it as He wills.

There are two ways in which God has chosen to communicate with humanity. The first is through the creation of the universe. From the beginning of our existence, human beings have been born into the world and have seen it in all of its magnificence. From the mountains, to the sky, to the trees, to other human beings that surround us, we are compelled to conclude that it originated in the mind of this all powerful, creative being. This is what theologians have often called "general revelation" (Romans 1:20).

While creation is the universal way in which humanity experiences the voice of God, it is not the primary way for one who seeks to have a deeper relationship with his creator. This moves us to the most foundational way in which Christians come to know the nature and personality of their creator—the Bible. The Christian sees history as a time in which God has, at different times and ages, decided to step into His creation and speak to certain individuals. These individuals would eventually come to record His divine words. It began with the first humans and then continued on. It spanned the history of Israel and continued into the age of the early church as the Apostles wrote down the teachings of Christ Himself.

Eventually the canon of Scripture was closed, and it became the final authority for all of Christian life and practice (2 Timothy 3:16). This is the way in which Christians manage the reality that is put before them. Like all other human beings, Christians experience subjective reality. For them, Scripture is what points them to the objective reality of God. It is the means by which they interpret their subjective reality and come to rest on the objective. It is how they walk in unity in the midst of all their God-ordained diversity.

Interpretation

This leads to a very difficult question. How do Christians rely on the objective Scriptures when they all experience them subjectively? To answer this, another element of the Christian world-view must be explained. In the mind and heart of the Christian, it is assumed that the Spirit of God is working from the very beginning of the Christian walk. When a human being comes to know God, the Spirit of God opens his or her mind to understand the Scriptures (1 Corinthians 2:13).

All that being said, it certainly does not mean that Christians will always agree. Remnants of our old mindset, from before we came to know the Lord, still influence our understanding. We are continuing to grow and to allow our minds to be formed into that which perceives spiritual reality. However slow that growth may be, it is sure to happen when God is at work. God promises to give us understanding (2 Timothy 2:7). As we struggle to understand the Word of God, we can rest assured that He has already begun a work in us.

As wonderful as this may sound, how does it play out practically? How does one come to know that he or she is coming closer to the true meaning of God's Word? While we can rest assured that the Spirit of God will assist us, there are some practical steps and common sense methods that we can take into account as we approach the Word of God.

It is very helpful to understand the concept of genre when approaching the text of Scripture. Different portions of scripture must be read with different mind-sets. Some portions are historical. Some are narratives. Some are poetic. Some are theologically instructive. Some are apocalyptic and symbolic. These are sometimes easily discernible, yet sometimes one may need to seek out the opinion of a Study Bible or some other type of book that outlines the different forms of biblical literature.

Also, one must understand the unity as well as the diversity of scripture. While the diversity of the text is certainly expressed in genre, the text was also written over thousands of years by many different authors. Different texts address many different times and situations. It can often be a difficult task to discover what each time and situation was. At times a misunderstanding of these factors can lead to a misunderstanding of the meaning of the text.

While the text is certainly diverse, it must also be understood that the Bible is unified in a very profound way. Christians believe that the construction of the Bible was not a random set of events in history. It was planned and guided by God. This leads to a few very important presuppositions with which a faithful Christian must approach the text.

First, harmony exists within all the diverse aspects of the Bible. While certain texts may stand in stark contrast with each other, we must approach them with a mind to see how we can find balance between them. We should see these tensions as ways with which God has invited us to know the varying aspects of His nature. God's thoughts and ways of communicating come from a mind that created the universe; we can't expect to understand what He reveals in one glance.

Second, the Bible is without error in all that it teaches insofar as it is faithfully translated from the original Greek and Hebrew texts, and insofar as those texts have been faithfully assembled. If indeed God inspired the text of Scripture, we should expect that it be consistent with itself and with the truths that it represents. If God Himself is without error, then His words ought to take on this characteristic as well.

That being said, we must explain what we mean by "without error." We must take into account what has been said already. For example, Scripture comes in many different genres. Some texts communicate stories in which people err, or lie. Some poetry exaggerates and uses hyperbole. It takes on the characteristics of the many human authors God used. This does not mean the Scripture is itself erring, but that it is communicating truth through that narrative or through that poetic and symbolic means. Not all scholars agree on the genres and means by which the Bible is communicating in all texts. Even so, we must agree that when the truth that the Bible is attempting to communicate is discerned, it must be believed. This is what makes it our foundation. If a human being takes it in his or her hands to call the truth of Scripture "error," that person must think he or she has another foundation with which to hold the Scriptures up to scrutiny. If it is the word of God, this is pride of the most profound sort.

Doctrine

In the end, we can take some comfort. The Bible in its present form has existed for nearly two thousand years. We are not the first to attempt to discern its meaning. As the Church has moved throughout her history, her understanding of the Bible has solidified in many ways. There is a great wealth of writings from every era with which we can see the way our fathers and mothers in the faith have agreed and disagreed over certain issues of interpretation. This is the way in which Christian doctrine has been formed throughout the centuries. While all doctrine should, in principle, be correctable by Scripture, we should be open to letting the understanding of those who came before us help our reading of the text.

This book is an attempt to bring together a coherent vision of the way a Christian can interpret the narrative of Scripture and therefore his or her life in the midst of it. This was the hope of the Apostle Paul as he instructed his friend Timothy concerning his walk with God in the journey toward understanding. He saw doctrine and life as inseparable (1 Timothy 4:16).

Recommended Reading

Bibles, Crossway *Esv Study Bible: English* Standard Version. ESV text ed. Wheaton, Ill.: Crossway, 2008.)

Comfort, Philip W., ed. *The Origin of the Bible.* Wheaton, Ill.: Tyndale House Publishers, Inc., 2003.

Grudem, Wayne. *Systematic Theology: an Introduction to Biblical Doctrine*. Grand Rapids, Mich.: Zondervan, 1994.

McGrath, Alister E. *Historical Theology: an Introduction to the History of Christian Thought.* Oxford: Wiley-Blackwell, 1998.

Piper, John. *Think: the Life of the Mind and the Love of God.* Reprint ed. Wheaton: Crossway, 2011.

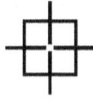

God

No Religion has ever been greater than its idea of God.[1]

~A.W. Tozer

With a foundation for Biblical doctrine in place, we are now in a position to begin looking into just what those foundational doctrines are and how we can come to see them in Scripture. What better place to start than with God Himself—the main character of Scripture. This chapter will be put under two main headings. The first will be who God is in terms of His being. This will mainly cover the concept of God's triune nature. The second will be the attributes of God. This has more to do with God's personality and qualities.

Trinity

From the start of the Church's history, Christians have worked very hard to preserve the nature of God in a doctrinal form. Because of the difficulty and complexity of the way God reveals Himself in Scripture, the earliest Christians were forced to define God's nature in some very

---

[1] A.W. Tozer, *The Knowledge of the Holy: the Attributes of God, Their Meaning in the Christian Life* (San Francisco: HarperOne, 1978), 9.

difficult and sometimes controversial ways. This is most plainly shown in the doctrine of the Trinity.

While it is certainly true that the triune nature of God is clarified as the Bible progresses, there are clues to some of the mysteriously distinct aspects of God's nature throughout Scripture, even in the Old Testament (OT) if one reads it very closely. There are times in which the "Spirit" of God is mentioned in a distinct way (Genesis 1:2). There are times in which the "Angel" of the Lord is mentioned as a distinct being and yet seems to take on the identity of God Himself (Genesis 16:7, 10-11, 13; 18:1-33; Exodus 3:1-4:31; 32:20-22; Numbers 22:35. 38; Judges 2:1-2; 6:11-18). There are also Jewish traditions before the writing of the New Testament (NT) which see the "Word" of God as a separate, yet fully divine creative agent. This may in fact be the roots from which John 1:1-18 sprang.

The doctrine of the Trinity becomes much clearer in the NT. While the word "Trinity" cannot be found in the Bible, the necessity of such a concept becomes very clear as one looks at the way in which God reveals and describes Himself, particularly through Christ's teaching. The great commission itself (which we will cover in chapter 7) commands baptism to be done in the name of the Father, the Son, and the Holy Spirit (Matthew 28:19). While the Father is always called God, there are also explicit references to Christ as God in several places (John 1:1, 14, 20:28; Romans 9:5; Philippians 2:5-7; Titus 2:13; Hebrews 1:3, 8,

10; 2 Peter 1:1). Not only that, but the Spirit is a term used interchangeably with God throughout the Bible making the Spirit's deity implicit. There is also Scripture where it is made explicit (2 Corinthians 3:17-18).

The controversy surrounding this mysterious concept intensified throughout the first few centuries of the early church. It took a while for a full doctrinal formula to be finalized by orthodox Christians. In the end there was a set of truths that was finally settled as being foundational to the doctrine of the trinity: There is one God. The Father is God. The Son is God. The Spirit is God. The Father is not the Son or the Spirit. The Son is not the Father or the Spirit. The Spirit is not the Father or the Son. They are all distinct persons, or centers of consciousness, which exist in one essence, or being, simultaneously. They are not three and one in the same sense, but are three in one sense and one in another.

Possible Errors

Obviously there is great mystery involved in this doctrine, but to deny that it is biblical would be to ignore a great number of explicit Scriptures. Because of the difficulty of this doctrine as well as the corruption and finite nature of the human mind, many heresies have arisen surrounding the Trinity throughout church history. A few are worth mentioning. There are three ways we will cover in which the doctrine of the trinity is usually corrupted. First, one or more members of the Trinity is demoted to a lesser place than deity, either partially or totally. Second, the distinction of the three persons is denied. Third, the unity of the three persons is denied.

The first error mentioned expressed itself in the early church in the heresy known as Arianism. It was this teaching that denied the deity of Christ and claimed that He was a created being rather than co-eternal with the Father. This led to a great deal of dispute before it was finally settled. Today, there is a similar teaching among the Jehovah's Witnesses. They claim that Christ is not divine, but is created. They also deny that the Holy Spirit is personal, let alone God Himself. This has led to many irresponsible and even intentional mis-translations in the New World Translation (the scripture the Jehovah's Witnesses use). While Arianism is a part of the distant past, this proves that old errors still manifest themselves today in new ways.

The second error mentioned is usually manifested in what is called "modalism." This teaching denies that the being of God exists in three distinct persons. Ultimately they see the three persons of the Trinity as three different "modes" with which God manifests Himself. This has also been called "oneness" theology or "Jesus only." The problems with this should become obvious as the narrative of Scripture is considered. For example, at the baptism of Christ, all three members of the Trinity were present. Also, it wouldn't make sense for Christ to have prayed to his Father before His death (Matthew 26) or throughout His life preceding it if the persons of the Trinity were not distinct. Beyond this, it wouldn't make sense to say that the Father or Spirit died on the cross. The Son died on the Cross and then committed His spirit to the Father (Luke 23:46).

Finally, there are some who may deny that the three persons truly exist in one being or essence. These would be called polytheists. This goes against orthodox theology from the very beginning of its history. One could say that the Mormons fit under this category. In their theology, they teach that humanity is uncreated, but only progresses until it moves into the status of deity. They claim that Christ was one who did this. Rather than being God who became a man, Christ is seen as a man who became a god. This form of existence is applied to all beings, including God Himself. Ultimately, God is seen as a human being who has achieved deity and perfection. Therefore, not only is the unity of Christ and the Father removed, but the distinction between humanity and deity is, in principle, inevitably removed. Humans are seen as gods in embryo form.

Examples such as these show ways in which carnal thinking can bring us into gross biblical error. The mind of the Christian must keep itself in constant check so that it is always submitted to the true teaching of Scripture. Room must be made for correction and submission to the teachings of the church which have come before.

The Attributes of God

Theologians have in times past found it helpful to place the attributes of God under two different headings. First, there are the *incommunicable* attributes of God. These are the attributes of God that will never be shared with His creatures. Second, there are the *communicable* attributes of God. These can either be shared with humanity, or they affect the lives of God's people in some way as we gain understanding of His nature.

First among God's incommunicable attributes is His eternal nature. He is without beginning and end. He is beyond time and brought time into existence (Psalms 90:2; Exodus 3:14; Job 36:26; Psalms 90:4; Isaiah 46:9-10; John 8:58; 1 Timothy 6:16; 2 Peter 3:8; Jude 24-25; Revelation 1:8; 4:8).

Second, He is entirely independent of His creation. He did not create the universe out of a lack that existed within Himself but creation was an overflow of His generous, self-existent, self-relating, and triune nature. God did not create the universe because He lacked something to love. Love has existed within the Trinity from all eternity (Acts 17:24-25; Exodus 3:14; Job 41:11; Psalms 50:9-12; 90:2).

Third, God is immutable. He is incapable of changing His nature. He is true to His plans and covenants and commitments (Malachi 3:6; Psalms 102:25-27; James 1:17; Psalms 33:11; Isaiah 46:9-11; Numbers 23:19; Romans 11:29).

Fourth, He is omnipresent. As creator of the universe, He inhabits every place within it. There is nowhere we can go to escape His vision and rule (Jeremiah 23:23-24; 1 Kings 8:27; Psalms 139:7-10; Isaiah 66:1-2; Acts 7:48-50).

In the category of the communicable attributes of God, we will name seven characteristics. These will be described a bit more since they are more applicable to our everyday lives. First, God is Holy. This is true in the sense that He is without flaw. However, since this can also be said of any being who is without sin, such as the angels who did not rebel with satan, it must also be true in that He is and always will be without equal. He is entirely *other*. However, in many ways, He wishes to communicate His holiness to us in order that we would become more like Him (Revelation 4:8, Exodus 15:11; 1 Chronicles 16:27-29; Isaiah 57:15; Isaiah 5:16; 6:1-8; Acts 3:14; Hebrews 7:26).

Second, God is loving. Not only does love exist within the Trinity, but God loves His creation. He loves and redeems sinners. He changes us that we might love one another. We are to know God in His love and allow that love to penetrate our hearts that we would demonstrate it to the world. This is demonstrated chiefly in Christ as He gave His life for His people on the cross (1 John 4:8-10; John 3:16; 15:13; 17:24; Romans 5:8; 8:31-39; Galatians 2:20; 1 John 3:16; 4:16).

Third, God is wrathful. Since God is to be valued above all beings in the universe, when He is dishonored and disobeyed, and His love is scorned, He responds with holy wrath. This is rightly meant to merit fear in His creatures as He promises punishment which will be poured out for every sin—one way or another (Revelation 6:15-16; Exodus 34:7; Romans 1:18; 2:4; 2 Corinthians 5:10; 2 Thessalonians 1:5; 2 Peter 3:9).

Fourth, God is omniscient. As the creator of all that exists, He is aware of all that exists in His creation. Not only does He know it as it presently is, but He knows all that has ever been and what will be. God is aware of the past, present, and future. This should give us great comfort and bring us to a place of awe. God knows our lives from beginning to end. He is able to not only see our lives, but He has had made plans for them from the beginning. He is able to comfort us in the hardest of times (1 John 3:20; Job 28:24; 37:16; Psalms 139:1-3; 147:5; Isaiah 55:8-9; Matthew 10:29-30; Romans 11:33-34; 1 Corinthians 2:10-11; Hebrews 4:13).

Fifth, God is wise. Not only does God know all things, but He has wisdom in his dealings with all of reality. Not only does He act wisely, but He teaches wisdom through His word. He grants wisdom and understanding by the power of His Holy Spirit (Daniel 2:20; Job 9:4; 12:13; Psalms 104:24; Romans 11:33; 16:27; 1 Corinthians 1:21-29; Ephesians 3:10-11).

Sixth, God is omnipotent. Not only does God know all things and have the wisdom to make plans, but He has the power to accomplish every single one of those plans without exception. This should also bring us comfort as we rest in the knowledge that nothing is outside of God's powerful reach (Isaiah 46:9-10; Exodus 6:3; Job 37:23; 40:2; 42:1-6; Psalms 24:6; 33:10-11; 91:1; Daniel 4:34-35; Matthew 28:18).

Finally, God is sovereign. Not only is God all knowing, all wise, and all powerful, but not one element of any of these attributes goes to waste. Not one event is outside of God's knowledge and wise purpose. All things fall under God's rule and God's will. All things are foreknown and happen according to God's perfect plan (Proverbs 16:19, 21, 33; Matthew 10:29; Ephesians 1:11; Romans 8:28-30; 11:34-36).

To look throughout Scripture and to see the various ways in which God is described can be a truly life transforming experience. It is something that can provoke hope, fear, joy, love, zeal, or all of the above. God was not made with human hands and is not subject to any of His creatures. He rules heaven and earth, young and old, rich and poor. He deserves the allegiance of every individual. He is the hero of Scripture and the hero of His church.

Recommended Reading

Biblical Doctrine: An Overview (from the ESV Study Bible; See chapter 1 recommended reading)

Tozer, A. W. *The Knowledge of the Holy: the Attributes of God, Their Meaning in the Christian Life.* San Francisco: HarperOne, 1978.

White, James R. *Is the Mormon My Brother?* Birmingham, Ala.: Solid Ground Christian Books, 2008.

White, James R. *The Forgotten Trinity.* Minneapolis, Minn.: Bethany House Publishers, 1998.

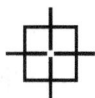

Creation

For his invisible attributes, namely, his eternal power and divine nature, have been clearly perceived, ever since the creation of the world in the things that have been made.

~Romans 1:20

The Genesis

"In the beginning God created..." (Genesis 1:1 emphasis added). So begins history. Now that the foundational aspects of God's character have been shown, we can begin looking at the way He has decided to reveal Himself. At the start of the Bible, we see God speak the world into existence. In a very poetic and progressive way, God begins forming different aspects of the universe. Over the course of six days, we see light come into existence. We see the heavens and the earth take their shape, oceans and land, plants and animals, and finally, humanity.

The first chapter of Genesis seems to be very straightforward for many Christians. Day one, day two, day three, and so on. God made the earth out of nothing, and so began our history. It is easy to skim over this account of creation and quickly think we understand all it means, yet this does not explain why there is such a great diversity of opinion concerning its meaning throughout church history.

As scientific discoveries have been made and theories have been developed, the truthfulness of this creation account has been called into question. If the earth was made in six days and this immediately began our human history, then why have so many scientists claimed that the earth is billions of years old? What does the theory of evolution bring to the table in this discussion? If these scientific theories bear any truth, should it effect our reading of Scripture or cause us to call its authority into question?

Some who hold modern scientific opinion in high regard do in fact look at Scripture and dismiss it as archaic. Some take this opportunity to dismiss its claims altogether. What are we to say to this? In the end, perhaps the Christian *will* have to make a choice. Will we allow the Holy Spirit's inner witness that the Bible is the Word of God hold sway as it is called into question, or will we allow another standard of truth to scrutinize the Bible?

This chapter is by no means meant to make broad scientific arguments to refute evolution. The ultimate aim of this chapter is to take a look at some different opinions concerning the meaning of Genesis 1 in order to see whether it is truly necessary to pit faith against science. If it is, then which scientific claims are irreconcilable with what the Scripture actually says? Which biblical interpretations are merely tradition and which should be maintained—with or without scientific agreement?

The Varying Perspectives and
How They Relate to the Fall of Humanity

Before we delve into the different opinions on this matter, it should be stated that all of them hold one belief in common. God created the heavens and the earth. While some of these positions are radically different from one another, this central truth is maintained.

Young Earth

A position that is broadly held by many conservative Christians is what might be called "literal, young earth, six day creationism." Those who hold to this position maintain that the six days are literal. They assert that, given the length of time which has passed since the creation, judging from biblical genealogies and history, the earth is somewhere between 6000 and 10,000 years old.

When confronted with what scientists interpret to be evidence to the contrary, some consider the idea that perhaps God created the world with the "appearance" of age. Just as Adam was created as an adult and had no actual birth, infancy, or childhood, perhaps God created the earth in a state of maturity as well. They may also attribute many of the signs of age to the Biblical account of the flood, since floods are capable of giving an appearance of sudden decay.

Old Earth Perspectives

Another perspective that is also becoming more common is what many call "old earth creationism." This perspective could be broken down into three different ways of thinking. First is what many have called "gap theory." While this perspective is not as popular as it once was, there are still some who hold to it. Those who hold to this opinion see the space between the first two verses of Genesis 1 as a possible gap in creation history. They theorize that perhaps God had a first creation which ultimately fell into destruction and, from verse 2 onward, God is starting over with a new humanity. This leaves room for an old earth, but a literal six days of creation.

Second under the heading of "old earth creationism" is what is called "historic creationism." It is called "historic" because those who hold to it claim that their theory is most probably closer to what Christianity taught up until the 1600s. It was in that century when James Usher, an arch-bishop, articulated young earth creationism as we often hear it today. Historic creationists hold to an understanding of Genesis 1:1 which sees the concept of "beginning" in Hebrew as referring to an indefinite period of time and therefore the age of the earth is unknown. While they don't speculate about a possible prehistory to the eventual six-day creation, they do maintain that the earth is old and the six days are literal. The days are simply seen as a forming and separating out of creation rather than a continued creation out of nothing. All of creation was finished in verse one.

Third under the heading of "old earth creationism" is the opinion that the days are not actually literal. This might be called "day/age" creationism. Those who hold to this position recognize that the word "day" in Hebrew can at times refer to a longer period of time. Therefore, they theorize that perhaps all six days took as much time as scientists might speculate to be the age of the earth, whether it be thousands, millions, or billions of years. This then ended with the creation of Adam and Eve and the beginning of human history.

Theistic Evolutionary Perspectives

The next way in which Christians have understood Genesis 1 is what might be called a "poetic" interpretation. Those that we will focus on are called "theistic evolutionists." Rather than saying that popular scientific opinion contradicts Scripture, they look at the first chapter of Genesis through the lens of a different genre. While the other positions hold to a historical Adam, many theistic evolutionists do not. Since the other positions we have already covered don't necessarily possess any danger of touching on central Christian doctrine, we will move on from them. This understanding, on the other hand, has the potential of calling some deeply held biblical truths into question.

One thing that should be mentioned before we continue is that Genesis 1 does indeed take on the characteristics of many of the poetic creation accounts of its day. There is also evidence that the genesis account contains similarities to historic accounts of what might be called a "functional inauguration" of a "cosmic temple" which a deity was believed to establish. This was common in many of the creation accounts outside of biblical literature. This doesn't so much concern the scientific theories that lie behind one's interpretation of Genesis 1, but how one is to understand the chapter in relationship to its historical context as well as to the rest of Scripture (for a full defense of this idea from history and scripture, read John Walton's *The Lost World of Genesis one*).

There are three ways in which a theistic evolutionist might articulate his or her position. Two of them may possess the theological elements to be considered orthodox, while one of them should most likely be rejected.

The first one we will mention holds to the idea that God used the process of evolution all the way up until the creation of Adam and Eve. It was then that God decided to do something different. While all other living things were brought about progressively (as science popularly claims), Adam and Eve were formed out of the dust of the Earth as Genesis 2 articulates. Therefore God used the process of evolution primarily, and yet humanity is still understood to be young.

The second way a theistic evolutionist might articulate his or her position is that humanity did in fact come about through the process of evolution. However, a time eventually came where the head of a human tribe named Adam was declared to be an image bearer of God. Therefore, all of Genesis 1-2 is, in some sense, symbolic. However, Adam is still historical. Therefore, when Adam fell, his sin was accounted to the rest of humanity corporately since Adam was their representative and sin spread throughout history from that point forward. The reason this could possibly still be seen as orthodox is that it might have some ability to maintain a point that Paul eventually makes in the book of Romans. It does so in a way that the final position we will mention in a moment does not.

The point we are talking about is not only the historical nature of Adam, but the parallel he holds to Christ. Just as sin entered the world through a truly historical man, a truly historical Jesus breaks the curse on the cross. This is the point that Paul clearly outlines in Romans chapter 5. While some may say that sin could only continue through physical lineage and therefore Adam had to be the very first man that existed, one who holds this perspective might point out that we are not physically descended from Christ either. His righteousness is accounted to those who are united to Him and it is imparted spiritually, just as this model would articulate to be the case with Adam's sin.

They might defend the idea of a corporate fall by pointing out that among the first children that are mentioned as being conceived by Adam and Eve, Cain says something very interesting. After the murder of his brother in Genesis chapter 4, he is cursed to wander the Earth. When this happens, Cain expresses his fear that he might be killed by those he stumbles across in his wanderings. Who would he stumble across if he is wandering away from the first family on the entire planet? While those in some of the other perspectives may have responses to this, it is certainly worth thinking about. What is important is that this position maintains a literal, historical Adam, a literal fall (though it is spread spiritually), and a theological parallel maintained between Adam and Christ.

While some may find the view just articulated questionable, they will most definitely object to the final one we will explain—and they should. While the idea of a corporate fall may push biblical theology to its limit, this next way of understanding takes it over the edge and outside of acceptable theology. This final form of theistic evolution not only maintains that humans came about through evolution, but they reject a literal Adam and a literal fall. They usually maintain the idea that the fall merely symbolized a personal fall into sin that we all make. While this acknowledges sin that needs to be dealt with, it destroys the crucial parallel or "typology" between Adam and Christ. In the same way that sin is passed on through one historical man's fall, a historical Christ's obedience is passed on as the solution to that fall.

Redemptive history hangs on historical people in the minds of biblical authors.

Conclusion

There are a few basic truths that should be understood and maintained as we interpret Genesis 1 and the chapters that follow. First, God is the creator of the universe. The cosmos is finite, while God is eternal. Second, Biblical authors understood Adam to be historical. Not only did they believe this doctrine, but they articulated other foundational doctrinal truths that spring up from it concerning sin and redemption. Finally, while the idea of evolution on its own may not immediately destroy the foundations of Christianity, there are implications of understanding it in certain ways that could be potentially devastating to an orthodox understanding of Christianity. The Scriptures do appear to teach that there was a historical Adam who was the first human and brought about the rest of the inhabited earth. While the concept of a "corporate" fall among a people led by Adam may stretch biblical theology to the breaking point, the rejection of *any* historical fall utterly shatters it.

The idea of a God who created the universe is deeply connected to the way we view the earth itself. It contributes to how we understand and view the natural world and it helps us to interpret our experience of that world. As you continue through the Biblical story and as you do your own study of the narrative of Scripture, this will help you to understand the mindset of the people who wrote the Bible as well as the characters in it.

Recommended Reading

Chesterton, G. K. *Orthodoxy*. Hollywood, FL: Simon & Brown, 2012.

Craig, William Lane. *Reasonable Faith*: Christian Truth and Apologetics. 3rd ed. Wheaton, Ill.: Crossway, 2008.

Keller, Timothy. *The Reason for God.* Reprint ed. New York: Riverhead, 2008.

Lewis, C S. *Mere Christianity*. New York: HarperCollins, 2011.

Walton, John H. *The Lost World of Genesis One: Ancient Cosmology and the Origins Debate*. Downers Grove, IL: IVP Academic, 2009.

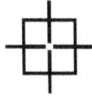

Humanity

Since we are all naturally prone to hypocrisy, any empty semblance of righteousness is quite enough to satisfy us instead of righteousness itself.[2]

~John Calvin

Who are We?

There are many ways we might approach arguing for the Christian faith. We may start with the historical evidence for the Bible. One may start with an argument from the creation we see around us every day. There are limitless ways we might argue from objective reality that there is a God and that the Bible is His Word. As convincing as many of these arguments may be, there is another way. There is a subjective argument that has the potential of penetrating to the core—should God so choose to open someone's heart to it. We will get to just what this argument is later in the chapter.

---

[2] John Calvin, *The Institutes of Christian Religion.* Book 1, Chapter 1, Section 2. www.ccel.org.

Many Christians try to start their defense of the gospel from scratch, as if there is no part of the human heart that considers spiritual reality apart from being evangelized. This leaves a very important element of the biblical narrative unconsidered. At the start of creation, Scripture describes humanity in a very unique way. At the start, scripture claims: "God created man in His own image, in the image of God he created him; male and female he created them" (Genesis 1:27).

What does it mean to be made in the image of God? Theologians have debated this question for generations. There are a great many directions that one could go with such a profound statement. Perhaps one of the most intuitive inferences we could draw from this idea is that humanity is meant to *image* God. This doesn't seem like a great leap. What is an image? An image is the parallel of another reality. It is a picture, a portrait—a representation.

In the 1700s, during the great awakening in New England, there was a great theologian named Jonathan Edwards. He wrote a book that laid out philosophical as well as numerous scriptural arguments in order to explain why God made the universe, the earth, and the human race. His book was called "The End for Which God Created the World." It is his conclusion that God made the human race along with all of creation to glorify Himself above all things. In response to the most intuitive question "isn't this a very self-seeking thing for God to do?" Edwards argues in his writings that the most virtuous thing a being could ever do is value that which is most valuable.

What is the most valuable thing in the universe? Or better yet, *who* is the most valuable *person*? Among humanity, great conflict arises when one human being lifts him or herself over another—when someone makes him or herself out to be more valuable that others. Why is this? Why does this result in conflict? Why do humans chafe at the idea of one human being lifted above all others? There are two ways in which we will address this question. One has to do with who God is, the other has to do with who we are, or better yet, who we have become.

A Mission Failed

From the start of creation, we now see that there was one great mission which humanity was meant to accomplish. We were made to *image* God. This is the title He gave us. Images. Think for a moment about times in which humans have made images of themselves. What does this look like? We paint portraits. We build statues of our heroes. What is the point of this? Images are made to show the beauty and glory of what they represent. If God simply made statues of Himself and covered the Earth with them, what do you suppose the point would be? This is actually what God did. However, God is able to make statues that see, hear, reason, and comprehend His existence. God desires His existence to be known. He wants His glory to be seen. He not only wants it seen, but valued.

With this view of creation in mind, who is the most valuable being in the universe? Who would be a more likely candidate that the One who brought it all into existence. God created humanity for His glory. He placed Adam and Eve in the garden and gave them authority to rule it and tend it as His representatives. He brought them into being to let His ways and His character be known on the earth He created. This was our mission.

As Adam and Eve began their task in the garden, God gave them one rule. They were not to eat of the Tree of Knowledge of good and evil. He warned them that if they did, they would die that very day. Outside of this, they were free to eat of any other tree. They had access to what was called "The Tree of Life." This was how their existence began.

However, this way of life did not continue forever. There came a day when one of God's creatures found it in his heart to deceive God's image bearers. This creature was the serpent. He approached Eve in the garden and began to guide her in the questioning of God's commands. He convinced her that God didn't have her best interests at heart. He told her that the forbidden tree was, in fact, exactly what she wanted. However, what was the foundational lie that he told her? In Genesis 3 we find the answer: "You will not surely die. For God knows that when you eat of it your eyes will be opened, and you will be like God, knowing good and evil" (Genesis 3:4-5).

What do we see in this exchange? We see the serpent make an offer to Eve. He tells her that she will cease to exist in the human state she is in. He tells her that she can become much more. He tells her that she can be like God Himself. As a result, she eats from the tree. She then turns to her husband who has been with her in the midst of the entire situation, and he eats as well.

As we discover in the very next chapters of scripture and as we briefly mentioned in the last chapter, death begins to spread from that very moment. We begin to see humanity continue to act as if they desire to bring themselves to greater positions of power. They don't merely wish to be higher than God—they desire to be greater than one another. They cease to glorify God as they should and try to glorify themselves—a circular and fruitless endeavor.

This raises a question. Why does it seem that God did not keep His word? Didn't He say that Adam and Eve would die on the very day they ate the fruit? Did God simply decide to show mercy? While God does prove to be merciful throughout Scripture, a theme we will touch on later, at no point does God ultimately contradict His Word.

The answer to this question is not blatantly answered until much later in the Bible. As we read the writings of the Apostle Paul, we see him say something very interesting about the nature of disobeying God. In the book of Romans, Paul dedicates the entire first three chapters to explaining the depraved state of humanity after the fall of Adam and Eve.

He describes us as the most wicked creatures imaginable. Later in the book, he begins to describe his own experience as he encounters the commands of God in his own sinful state. He says, "I was once alive apart from the law, but when the commandment came, sin came alive and I died" (Romans 7:9).

This is an odd statement. It should be most obvious that a living man wrote this letter. Yet he speaks of a time in his life when he died. He died the day that sin came alive in him and he broke the commands of God. What is the death he is speaking of? There is another passage in the same book, in the very next chapter, that might give us a clue. A point comes when Paul says to the Christians he is writing to,

> You, however, are not in the flesh but in
> the Spirit, if in fact the Spirit of God dwells
> in you. Anyone who does not have the Spirit
> of Christ does not belong to him.
>
> (Romans 8:9)

It is in this portion of scripture that Paul contrasts those who do not belong to Christ and are in the flesh to those who do belong to Him and are of the Spirit. What does it mean to be of the flesh? Clearly it means those still living according to the sinful nature we have been describing. This means that they lack the Spirit. It is likely that the death Paul is speaking of is a spiritual death. The day that Adam and Eve disobeyed God, they died spiritually. We who now live according to our Adamic, sinful nature, are spiritually dead.

Our Two Great Problems

We will now begin to answer the question of just what it is that makes humans hate it when another human is lifted above them. What is it that causes us to seek our own glory? The answer is in the reality we have been describing in this chapter. From the very beginning we have been on a mission to dethrone God. If we can't stand to see someone on the throne who deserves to be there, then how could we ever stand to see someone there who doesn't deserve it? We are rebels to the very core.

This leads to two profound problems that Paul mentions in the first three chapters of Romans. It is here that Paul begins to lay out our state of existence. When describing us, he says,

> What can be known about God is plain to them, because God has shown it to them. For his invisible attributes have been clearly perceived, ever since the creation of the world in the things that have been made. So they are without excuse.

(Romans 1:19-20)

It is in this passage that we see Paul make one definitive statement. Human beings know that God exists. He doesn't say that God is hiding. He doesn't say that humanity is confused. He says that we all know in our heart of hearts that there is a creator. This is the first problem. What is the second?

In the next few verses, we see Paul make another statement. "For although they knew God, they did not honor him as God or give thanks to him, but they became futile in their thinking, and their foolish hearts were darkened" (Romans 1:21). This is only the beginning of the dark picture that Paul begins to draw. At the start of this description, Paul had indeed made the state of humanity clear. "For the wrath of God is revealed from heaven against all the ungodliness and unrighteousness of men, who by their unrighteousness suppress the truth" (Romans 1:18).

The second truth that Paul makes clear is not simply that humanity knows the truth, it *hates* the truth. He is confident enough to apply this description to the entire human race in the past tense. He knows in his heart that all of humanity is hostile toward God, and that God is hostile in return. He doesn't only say that the wrath of God will eventually be poured out, as he certainly does in other places, but he says it has already begun. He has handed us over to our own foolishness (v. 24).

A Profound Problem and a Profound Solution

I mentioned at the start that there was an excellent way to share the truth with others about the Christian faith. How have I presented such a way? Perhaps the most simple thing we can do as we speak to others about Christ is simply believe the plain words of the Apostle Paul. He begins with the assumption that all human beings are aware that God exists. This is something that many of us do not believe.

Entire books have been written by people who claim to have scientifically proven that there is no God. They have come up with their own lovely title—*atheist*. Paul paints a very different picture. At bottom, there is no such thing as an atheist. Everyone is aware of God—they simply suppress the truth. They either suppress the thought of His existence, or they suppress the righteousness of His nature and repaint Him in their own limited and marred image.

This is our state apart from God. We are haters of His commands. We are lovers of our sin. We go out of our way to invent ways of doing evil. This should be no surprise having finished what is recorded to be the bloodiest century in the history of the world. We have fought war after war around the world. We have been through racism, hatred, and despair. Yet every day we puff ourselves up and blame our problems on others.

We may not see the worst of our nature at all times and in all places, but we know our own hearts if we are honest with ourselves. While we may do good to other human beings, we know that our motives are always corrupted with pride and self promotion. While good may be accomplished at a horizontal level between one human and another, God looks down and knows what motivates each one of us. There is no hope of vertical righteousness—a righteousness in the eyes of God. Nothing is truly done for His glory.

This is our state. We were once in a state of perfection, yet somehow we found it in our hearts to break the commands of God in our forefather Adam. We value ourselves as individuals above everything and find God's righteous valuing of His own glory to be repulsive. We no longer image Him as we should and there is no part of our heart that seeks Him on its own (Romans 3:11). O dreadful people that we are, what will save us from this evil state we are in (Romans 7:24)?

This is the question we will be answering in the next two chapters, where a great deal of our time will be spent.

Recommended Reading

Edwards, Jonathan. *The Nature of True Virtue*. Reprint ed. Eugene, OR: Wipf & Stock Pub, 2003.

Luther, Martin. *The Bondage of the Will*. Philadelphia: Empire Books, 2012.

Platt, David. *Radical: Taking Back Your Faith from the American Dream*. Colorado Springs, Colo.: Multnomah Books, 2010.

Piper, John. *God's Passion for His Glory: Living the Vision of Jonathan Edwards* (with the Complete Text of the End for Which God Created the World). Wheaton: Crossway, 2006.

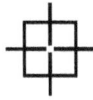

The Cross

> We needed one, the worthiness of
> whose obedience might be answerable to the
> unworthiness of our disobedience; and therefore
> needed one who was as great and worthy as we
> were unworthy.[3]
>
> ~Jonathan Edwards

The Need

In the last chapter, we looked at the incredibly devastating state of humanity since the fall of Adam and Eve. We have only looked in passing at what the solution might be. Who is this Jesus? What does the history of His life as a *parallel* to Adam truly mean?

The book of Romans is perhaps known for being the most thorough and explicit explanation of what the gospel of Jesus Christ is. This is where a great deal of our study will rest, both in this chapter and the next, though we will certainly reach into other books of the Bible.

After nearly three chapters in which Paul puts forward the most scathing critique of the state of the human race, he suddenly begins a new train of thought. He begins

---

[3] Jonathan Edwards, *The Works of Jonathan Edwards, Volume 1,* www.ccel.org, pg. 628.

to speak of a new way in which God's righteousness is revealed to the world. In the Old Testament, God revealed His righteousness through the law. He gave rule after rule, standard upon standard. Yet, after showing this, Paul even directs his criticism toward those who were given the law most directly and most clearly—the Jews. He finishes his condemnation of the entire human race by saying that both Jews and non-Jews are under sin in God's eyes. He sums this up by stating, "By the works of the law no human being will be justified in his sight, since through the law comes knowledge of sin" (Romans 3:20).

The Fulfillment

How on earth could a statement like this possibly be helpful? Don't we need to overcome our state and make up for the numerous failures that have separated us from God? Isn't this how any system of justice works in our world? Perhaps. Yet Paul seems to think that all hope is lost. He doesn't leave any power of salvation in the hands of wicked people. He seems to be leading the minds of his readers to another way. To begin to gain an understanding of the answer to which Paul is trying to bring us, we will quote the next section from him at length. In the following verses, he states:

> But now the righteousness of God has been manifested apart from the law, although the Law and the Prophets bear witness to it—the righteousness of God through faith in Jesus

Christ for all who believe. For there is no distinction: for all have sinned and fall short of the glory of God, and are *justified* freely by his grace as a gift, through the redemption that is in Christ Jesus, whom God put forward as a *propitiation* by his blood, to be received by *faith*. This was to show God's righteousness, because in his divine forbearance he had passed over former sins. It was to show his righteousness at the present time, so that he might be *just* and the *justifier* of the one who has faith in Jesus.

(Romans 3:21-26 emphasis added)

This is a very compact set of ideas that Paul is trying to explain in such a small section of scripture. What is it that he is trying to say? What hope does this give to humanity in its state of rebellion? What Paul has begun to show is that even though the Jews have been hearers of the law from the birth of their nation, they have not been doers of the law. The Jews' national identity does not save them from the fact that they have not lived up to the standard of the law—the only way they could be justified by the law (Romans 2:13). This shows that Paul's first intention is to put *all* people in *all* places in the *same* place—a place in which we despair of our self reliance.

What is Paul's next point? He begins his argument by showing that another righteousness has been revealed. A righteousness that is by *faith*. Paul is giving a new means to righteousness, a means that is available to all peoples without racial distinction. Racial distinction has proven to make no difference in whether one fulfills the law, therefore there is a new way into righteousness which has no bearing on where one has been born or what one has done. All have fallen short of God's standard and need a way that is independent of that standard.

There are two words from this passage that must be explained. The first is *justification*. The second is *propitiation*. We will begin with *justification*. There is something about this word in its original Greek form that does not show up in English. In actual fact, it comes from the same root as the word *righteousness*. When Paul speaks of God being *just* and God being *righteous*, he is ultimately saying the same thing. How does this relate to the passage at hand? It is important because Paul is clearly putting a lot of importance on the concept of God being *righteous*—especially toward the end of the passage. Paul says that there was something God did to show this righteousness. He put forward Jesus Christ as a *propitiation*. Before we discuss what *propitiation* means, we should first understand why God wished to show his righteousness. Paul says that "In his divine forbearance, he had passed over former sins" (v. 25).

So, why exactly does God's passing over former sins (the many sins in the Old Testament) result in Him needing to demonstrate His righteousness in any particular way—whether it be this thing called *propitiation* or something else? This leads us to look again at some of the scriptural truths that we explained in the last chapter. What is the nature of true virtue? What is the nature of righteousness? If indeed righteousness is to value that which is most valuable, then what is it to be unrighteous? How exactly is it that Paul describes sin—particularly in this passage? Remember what he writes. "All have sinned and fall short of the glory of God" (Romans 3:23). This is quite profound.

What is incredibly important for a reader of this text to notice is the unbreakable connection sin has to the glory of God. In Old Testament language, the *glory* of God is meant to communicate the incredible weight of His being— the profound nature of His essence. Therefore, if God is so weighty, or valuable, it would make sense that Paul would connect sin to the glory of God. To sin is to fall short of valuing God for all that He is. To sin is to put any created thing above its creator. If this is true, then what would God be saying if He passed over this thing called sin? The answer should be quite obvious. He would be sending a message that He Himself did not value that which is most valuable.

The Cross

For God to pass over those who break His laws and therefore call into the question the value of His perfect character would make God unrighteous. Therefore, God had to do something to show that He was and *is* righteous. This leads us to the next question. What is this thing called *propitiation*?

Throughout the history of biblical translation, this word has been translated in different ways. What many of the translations fail to take into account is the fact that Paul is trying to address the problem of divine wrath. Some translations communicate a separation of the sinner from his or her sin or a cleansing from unrighteousness (*expiation*), but only the term *propitiation* communicates what Paul is saying about the effect the putting forward of Christ had on God the Father. *Propitiation* is the only word that recognizes that Paul is making the heart of God toward sinners the focus. God must satisfy His just wrath toward sin. What is *propitiation*? It is the act that makes God *propitious* or *favorable.*

In the Old Testament, God made provision for the many times that His people sinned. He had an offering system by which the sinner would put his or her hand on the head of an animal and it symbolized the passing of his or her guilt onto that animal. The animal was then killed. This offering was meant to satisfy God's justice and wrath. What is made clear in the New Testament, particularly in the book of Hebrews, is that these sacrifices were only a picture of a greater reality to come. They were insufficient in and of themselves (Hebrews 10:4).

This leads to the ultimate question. What was the cross of Jesus Christ? Why do so many preachers believe it helps in some way? Why is it given such focus in the Christian faith? Because it is the fulfillment of every symbol in the Old Testament. Jesus Christ, who came to earth, took on flesh, and existed perfectly as both God and man, truly took our guilt upon Himself. He lived a sinless life. He needed to be pure and spotless like God commanded those sacrificial animals to be. He then was hated among humanity and arrested. He was beaten, scourged, and spit upon. He was humiliated and shamed. He was then nailed to a cross by wicked men. Finally, he died.

We now have the definition of both the justification of man and the propitiation of God. Now that Christ has been put forward as a propitiation for the sins of God's people, we are declared righteous in the sight of God. Much like a debt being paid and a sum being *credited* or *imputed* to our account, God now sees us as having the *righteousness* of Christ while punishing our sins on the the *cross* of Christ.

There is another truth about the cross that must now be made clear, and that is what Paul says about this final sacrifice. While wicked men carried out the brutal death of Jesus, it was not the whole story. This was not a random turn of events. What is most profound about this story is that it flowed from the plans that God had made before the foundations of the earth. We humans didn't set the plan of Christ's death in motion, God did. We didn't put Christ forward as a sacrifice, God did. As Paul says, "whom *God* put forward as a propitiation by his blood (Romans 3:25, emphasis added)."

Back in the Old Testament, a prophet named Isaiah looked forward to this event. He foresaw that there would need to be someone to take the sins of God's people upon Himself. He saw that God would have to be the one to put this man forward. He speaks of a suffering servant and doesn't ultimately put the weight of his sufferings in the hands of a hostile humanity. He puts them in the hands of God.

> Surely he has borne our griefs and carried our sorrows; yet we esteemed him stricken, smitten by *God,* and afflicted. But he was wounded for our transgressions; he was crushed for our iniquities; upon him was the chastisement that brought us peace, and by his stripes we are healed.
>
> (Isaiah 53:4-5, emphasis added)

Later in the passage, Isaiah makes the role of God the Father in the sufferings of His divine Son even clearer. "Yet it was the will of the *LORD* to crush him; *he* has put him to grief; when his soul makes an offering for guilt" (Isaiah 53:10, emphasis added).

For anyone who is thinking honestly about the logic of this act of God, there should be a question coming to mind. God is the one who was offended by our sin. God is the one whose wrath must be propitiated. An offering must be made to *Him.* Yet in these passages, God is the one putting forward an offering. God is the one making satisfaction. How can this be true? Isn't God the one who is angry? How can it be that the the greatest act of love that could ever be imagined came from the heart that is more offended than any other heart in the universe? That is the ultimate question... and that is the gospel. It is God whose anger needed to be satisfied. At the same time it is God who loved His people so much that He put forward what was needed to satisfy that anger. Doesn't God hate sinners (Psalm 4:5)? Yes, look at the cross. Doesn't God love sinners? Yes, look at the cross.

This is the good news. God chose not to leave us in our sorry state. He sent His Son to earth and made provision for our sins. It wasn't an accident that Christ died. In fact, Peter makes the plans of God behind this act even clearer when he speaks to God saying:

> For truly in the city there were gathered together against your holy servant Jesus, whom you anointed, both Herod and Pontius Pilate, along with the Gentiles and the peoples of Israel, to do whatever your *hand* and your *plan* had *predestined* to take place.
>
> (Acts 4:27-28 emphasis added)

The Resurrection

This may make a lot of sense to us. The connection of Christ with Old Testament sacrifice might be the answer for our guilt. However, is that where the story ends? How do we know that this man named Jesus was in fact God in the flesh? How is it that we know He wasn't actually some man who made outrageous claims and then was killed and proven wrong? What made the disciples so bold in their proclamation of the dead man, Jesus Christ?

The answer is quite simple. Christ is not dead—not anymore. Throughout His life, Jesus spoke of what was to come. He often told His disciples that He was going to die and then three days later rise again. Yet there were blinders on their eyes. They weren't blessed with the understanding of all that He was saying to them. Therefore, when Christ finally did die, they inevitably fell into despair. Many went and hid. Peter returned to fishing. They must have come to the conclusion that it was all a big mistake. Yet, this wasn't the end of the story. We see in the gospel accounts that even though the tomb of Christ was guarded and He was confirmed dead on the day of His crucifixion, His place of burial was suddenly found to be empty. Not only that, but He suddenly began to appear to those who had followed Him. In the end, there were upwards of five hundred who claimed to have seen Him and heard Him speak.

If this is true, what does it mean for those who wish to put their faith in Him as Paul describes? There are a few foundational things that the resurrection of Christ tells us.

While we may put our faith in Christ for the forgiveness of our sins in this life, we know that a day will still come when we will die. Paul speaks of a time in which our spirit will be absent from the body and yet present with the Lord (2 Cor. 5:8). Will this be the way in which we will spend eternity? Christ's resurrection gives us hope for something greater. Paul speaks of Christ's resurrection in a very special way. In some of Paul's other writings, he speaks of Christ as "the firstborn from the dead" (Colossians 1:18). What does this mean? Later in the book of Romans, Paul speaks of our adoptions as the sons of God and the redemption of our bodies (Rom. 8:23). What does that mean? Paul is speaking of a time that is yet to come.

Romans chapter 8 is an incredible picture of what is coming. We are still in a world between worlds. For those of us who put our faith in Jesus Christ, while we have truly been redeemed, we remain in broken bodies. We look forward to the finishing of our redemption when Christ returns. If the resurrection of Christ is true, which history demonstrates powerfully, then we have hope that death will not be the end of our physical lives. It not only proves that there is life beyond death, but there is yet another stage of our salvation after heaven. Our bodies will be redeemed just as our souls have been redeemed.

However, is hope for the future all that we have? We may enjoy looking forward to a time when our bodies will be renewed and the past will be forgotten, but what about here and now? Should we simply continue to sin and watch our bodies rot until the day we die along with those who have no hope? No. Paul speaks of a present reality in the same chapter. He speaks of the work of the Spirit of God even in the present life of those who are His. Paul speaks of the present reality of the Holy Spirit living in those who follow Christ and belong to Him.

> If the Spirit of him who raised Jesus from the dead dwells in you, he who raised Christ Jesus from the dead will also give life to your mortal bodies through his Spirit who dwells in you.
>
> (Romans 8:11)

All of Life

Something should now be obvious as we close this chapter. The call to Christianity is a call that is meant to bring change to the entire life. Once we see the pitiful state of sin and death we are in, the beauty of grace as it is expressed through the cross should be incredibly clear. Not only do we gain a present peace with God through His work of sending Christ to die on the cross, but we have seen this work to be complete in Christ's resurrection from the dead.

Not only do we have a confirmation that *justification* and *propitiation* have been completed through the resurrection, but we have hope of our own resurrection. Not only do we have hope of a future resurrection, but we have hope that we can live a holy life that pleases God through the power of His Holy Spirit. The same Spirit that raised Christ can change us to be more like Him. The Cross and Resurrection are realities that address every aspect of our being.

Recommended Reading

Morris, Leon. *The Apostolic Preaching of the Cross.* 3rd ed. Grand Rapids: Wm. B. Eerdmans Publishing Co., 1955.

Sproul, R. C. *Saved from What?* Reprint ed. Wheaton Illinois: Crossway, 2010.

Piper, John. *Desiring God,* Revised Edition: Meditations of a Christian Hedonist. Rev Exp ed. Colorado Springs, Colo.: Multnomah Books, 2011.

Piper, John. *Seeing and Savoring Jesus Christ.* Wheaton Illinois: Crossway Book, 2004.

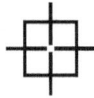

The Call

Human will does not by liberty obtain grace, but by grace obtains liberty.[4]

~John Calvin

The Question

What we have just explored is the foundation for all hope in the Christian life. God has made a way through the death of His Son for sinners like us to be saved from His wrath. Provision has been made. Faith in the person and work of Christ is the answer. However, for those who may have a knack for observation, there is a question that may have come to your minds as we have laid out these biblical truths.

The first thing that we explained was the rebellious state of the human heart. Apart from Christ, we have hearts that are hostile to God and all of His works. What the gospel offers is a way in which we can be reconciled. What this requires is a recognition that we are sinners. It requires repentance in order that we can turn to Him and submit in faith. This presents a problem. If the problem that keeps us

[4] John Calvin, *The Institutes of Christian Religion*. Book 2, Chapter 3, Section 14. www.ccel.org.

from God is a rebellious heart that will not submit, then why would God create a solution that requires us to submit and have a humble faith?

In this chapter we will be answering a question that has divided Christian thinkers throughout the entire history of the church. Because of this, the way in which we will present the Scriptures in the following pages will not land on all readers in the same way. Some will find the truths presented to be very difficult. Some will need to wrestle. Hopefully what is written will eventually take root and grow sweet in the soul of you who read and will give you a rock solid assurance that you belong to Christ and that He will keep you in His hands from now until we all meet Him at His return.

The Wisdom and Power of God

There is no doubt that throughout church history, as the gospel has been presented, there have been those who have found it to be beautiful and those who have turned away and found it to be foolish. The question is not *whether* this happens, but *why* it happens. What is it that causes the gospel to take root in one heart and not another? If you have accepted Christ, how is it that you explain the fact that you chose to submit to Christ and repent? What made the gospel beautiful to you?

Many people explain the different responses to the gospel by many different factors. Some say that we are raised in many different ways. We are raised in different places where we are taught different things. We all have different sources that feed into our lives until the day we hear the gospel. All these factors contribute to our response. This may sound reasonable, yet it doesn't take into account a very important truth that Paul presented in the book of Romans. As we saw in the previous chapters, all people are held captive by sin. Paul doesn't differentiate between them. In one particular place, he says plainly, "No one seeks for God" (Romans 3:11).

While we may be willing to recognize that we all are sinful and need Christ to save us, we seem to have no problem explaining our submission with human categories. We seem to think that our will is free from our sinful nature and we can turn it from evil to good without much effort. While we may not say so, there is no reason why this thinking shouldn't give us ground to boast in our willingness to place our faith in Christ. Is this the mindset that Paul offers us in his writings? Is this the mindset that Christ Himself had as He beckoned people to put their faith in Him? After Paul explains that our place of birth and our differing backgrounds have no meaningful connection to whether we fulfill the law, why would we use factors like this to explain how we come to submit and place our faith in Him?

It seems that a closer look at the biblical authors is most definitely in order. A good place to start may be in the first chapter of Paul's first letter to the Corinthians. It is here that he is speaking of his experience in preaching the gospel to all people groups. He comes to a point where he says:

> For Jews demand signs and Greeks seek wisdom, but we preach Christ crucified, a stumbling block to Jews and folly to Gentiles, but to those who are called, both Jews and Greeks, Christ the power of God and the wisdom of God.
>
> (1 Corinthians 1:22-24)

This passage presents a vision of the preaching of the gospel that is quite surprising. Paul claims to preach the gospel to all people groups without distinction. Yet he speaks of it being rejected by each of those groups without distinction as well. He then speaks of a group for whom it is the wisdom and power of God. These people come from among Jews and non Jews. What is it that made the difference? The secret may lie in one telling phrase: *those who are called* (v. 24). Many may look at this passage and automatically say that being called is the result of embracing the gospel, yet this would entirely ignore the problem we are facing. How is one who is by nature inclined to rebel against God going to fulfill the need for faith? How could someone change his or her heart to love the things of God and therefore be called? Paul seems to be making one's calling the *means* and not the *result* of this change of heart.

Looking at Romans chapter eight may give us even greater insight into this question. What is this *calling* that Paul writes about? There is an incredible verse in this chapter that gives many Christians great comfort. In it, Paul says, "We know that for those who love God all things work together for good, for those who are called according to his purpose" (Romans 8:28). It is here that we find Paul using this idea of *calling* yet again. What does he mean? Is being called simply a *result* of putting one's faith in Christ?

The following verses are incredibly helpful in explaining what Paul is saying when he speaks of the idea of calling and yet it is one of the most neglected passages of scripture for many Christians. In the following verses, Paul continues:

> For those whom he foreknew he also predestined to be conformed to the image of his Son, in order that he might be the firstborn among many brothers. And those whom he predestined he also called, and those whom he called he also justified, and those whom he justified he also glorified.
>
> (Romans 8:29-30)

He begins this amazing train of thought with the concept of *foreknowledge.* What does this word mean? Many Christians see this word and believe it is speaking of God's foresight of human beings placing their faith in Christ in order that He might call them. However, this does not stay true to the wording of the text or the biblical idea of God's *knowledge.* The text does not say that God is foreknowing peoples' *choices* or *faith.* It says that He is foreknowing *people.* What does Scripture mean when it speaks of God *knowing* a person?

The concept of God's personal knowledge originates in the Old Testament. There are times at which it applies to relationships between different people, but much of the time it refers to God and His people. In one of God's rebukes of His people in the Old Testament, He says, "You only have I *known* of all the families of the earth" (Amos 3:2, emphasis added). What does God mean by this? Does He mean that He is unaware of all other families or nations on the earth? No. Amos is alluding to the concept of divine love and relationship. Another place in which this concept can be found is when God initially began His work of creating a nation. In the book of Genesis, God speaks of Abraham saying,

> For I have *chosen* him that he may command his children and his household after him to keep the way of the LORD by doing righteousness and justice, so that the LORD may bring Abraham what he has promised him.

(Genesis 18:19 emphasis added)

There is no evidence here that Abraham was chosen because of any special merit that he possessed. But there is something very important that needs to be discussed concerning this translation from the original language.

What this translation conceals is the idea that lies behind the word *chosen* in Hebrew. This rendering is not a translation but an interpretation. The Hebrew word being translated is synonymous with the word *know*. That is not to say that the translation is bad, but to show that the concept of God knowing and God choosing are exactly the same in these passages. Therefore, since Paul is clearly writing of God's relationship to His people in Romans 8:29, we can most likely assume this is the concept Paul is referring to when he uses the word *foreknew*. Perhaps the best rendering would be to "lovingly choose beforehand." Another term Paul uses for this idea can be found just a few verses later when he says "Who shall bring any charge against God's *elect*?" (Romans 8:33, emphasis added)." Those whom God *chose* are those whom God *elected*.

On the basis of this election, Paul then speaks of God's predestination. One might say that God's foreknowledge is God's choosing of a person or people, while predestination is the work God decides to do on the basis of that choice. In this case, it is to bring those whom He predestines into conformity with the image of Christ. It then says that on the basis of this predestination, He *calls*. After all of this decision making that God does, He finally reaches the point at which He calls people to Himself. This is so backward in comparison to the way many intuitively think of the salvation process.

The Source of Faith and Repentance

Before we finish our study of this passage in Romans 8, we should look a bit deeper into another passage in which

Paul explains the concept of election. There are many who intuitively hold to the idea that God bases His election on what He foresees human beings choosing to do. Since God does know all things, past, present and future, one cannot deny that God foresees that people will have faith. The question is, does God *base* election on this knowledge?

In the following chapter of Romans, we see Paul begin to dig into the question of why so many Israelites have rejected their Messiah. Paul has presented the gospel to so many of his fellow Israelites. Why have they hardened their hearts? Does this mean that God's word has failed? It is from this point that Paul begins to respond to that very question. He writes,

> It is not as though the word of God has failed. For not all who are descended from Israel belong to Israel, and not all are children of Abraham because they are his offspring.
>
> (Romans 9:6)

It is here that we see Paul begin to speak of times in the history of Israel where God chose different children from among His followers. Later in the passage, after giving a few examples, he writes,

> And not only so, but also when Rebekah had conceived children by one man, our forefather Isaac, though they were not yet born and had done nothing either good or bad—in order that God's purpose of election might continue, not because of works but because of him who calls.
>
> (Romans 9:10-11)

It is here we see that while election does indeed take place before birth, it was not based on the good or evil God foresaw in the two brothers. It was done precisely so that it would not be based on this.

Some may say in response that election may not have been based on foreseen *works*, but on foreseen *faith*. While someone might boast in works, faith is what God wants. Yet Paul is not finished. Later in the passage he continues,

> What shall we say then? Is there injustice on God's part? By no means! For he says to Moses, I will have mercy on whom I have mercy, and I will have compassion on whom I have compassion. So then it depends not on human *will* or *exertion*, but on God who has mercy.
>
> (Romans 9:15-16, emphasis added)

While many of us are perfectly happy that we are not chosen on the basis of works, we still love to hold onto the idea that God chose us on the basis of our willingness to have faith. Yet, Paul says here that election is not based on one's *will* or any form of *exertion*. Besides, if Paul was attempting to contrast faith and works at this point, why begin by preempting the birth of those God elected in the first place?

Many may respond to this by asking, "I thought that faith was essential to my salvation. Didn't the last chapter show that we must put our faith in Jesus Christ to be saved?"

On the basis of many other passages, this is clearly true. Let's continue in *this* passage to see if we can find a clue that connects these two ideas. In the following verses, Paul writes,

> For the Scripture says to Pharaoh, "For this very purpose I have raised you up, that I might show my power in you, and that my name might be proclaimed in all the earth." So then he has mercy on whomever he wills, and he hardens whomever he wills.
>
> (Romans 9:17-18)

You might ask, how does this next section help the discussion? The clue lies in the contrast Paul makes between *mercy* and *hardening.* This seems like a very harsh concept. What does Paul mean? The trick is to look back at just what God did in His hardening of Pharaoh. One great reformer who did great theological work in explaining this concept was Martin Luther. In his book, "The Bondage of the Will," Luther explains the way God interacts with the sinner's heart. Since God does see the hardness of a sinner's heart, how is it that He accomplishes His plans? He has two choices. He can reach in and, in His grace, change that heart. Or, in His wrath, He can appeal to the sinful heart and command the sinner to repent, knowing full well that the one to whom He is appealing will turn away in rebellion. This is what God did with Pharaoh—ten times. It is through this interaction that

God allowed Pharaoh to show the guilt of his heart while at the same time fulfilling His plan to make His glory known.

Again, how does this help? Well, if the negative side of Paul's contrast is *hardening,* then what is the concept of *mercy* supposed to mean? It seems clear that if hardening is in the hands of God, then *softening* must be as well. This would mean that mercy and *repentance* are synonymous in these verses. This is made clear in several passages throughout Scripture. Paul in particular often refers to repentance and faith as gifts that God gives. In fact, it is clear that he gets this idea from Christ Himself.

In Paul's second letter to Timothy, he speaks of a church leader as one who should go about "correcting his opponents with gentleness." He then says, "God may perhaps *grant* them repentance leading to a knowledge of the truth" (2 Timothy 2:25, emphasis added). This seems odd. Paul places the task of correction in the hands of the minister, but then says that repentance is in the hands of God.

In the book of Ephesians, Paul places the entire work of salvation in the hands of God when he says, "For by grace you have been saved through faith. And this is not your own doing; it is the gift of God, not a result of works, so that no one may boast" (Ephesians 2:8-9). In the benediction of this same letter, he refers to faith in the same way as he says, "Peace be to the brothers, and love with *faith*, from God the Father and the Lord Jesus Christ" (Ephesians 6:23, emphasis added). This is also odd. Paul refers to faith, something usually considered a virtue produced by man, as something that comes from God along with love.

In the book of Romans itself, Paul exhorts his readers to be humble, but he does it in an interesting way. He writes, "Think with sober judgment, each according to the measure of faith that God has *assigned*" (Romans 12:3, emphasis added). As Paul looks at the people under his care, he knows that whatever virtue they have, God has assigned it with His own hand.

Finally, in the gospel of John, Jesus looks out at a crowd that is leaving Him and is hardened by His words and says, "No one can come to me unless it is granted him by the Father" (John 6:65).

The Nature of Human Will

How is it that we can understand God's interaction with the will in this way? What about the concept of *free will*? How are we to understand our relationship with God when the Bible seems to present our will in such a way? For many modern Christians, *free will* is seen as an attribute of human nature that operates independent of outside influences—though it is influenced by many things.

In contrast to this popular notion, it appears that biblical authors see the will as that which operates in *continuity* with the affections of the human being. This is called compatibilism. Human beings are always free to do that which they most desire, yet their desires always flow from their nature, which is determined by their forefather Adam. In this way of thinking, God is purposefully permitting humans to operate out of their sin nature, or He is, in His sovereign grace, awakening their affections to inevitably come to salvation both when He ordains and, as a result, when they desire. Therefore, according to this definition of the will, human beings are free to do what they desire and completely determined by God's sovereign will simultaneously. This position is defended very thoroughly by Jonathan Edwards in his book "The Freedom of the Will."

Many of us do not give much thought to the idea of what we mean by the concept of *free will*. All of our choices come from somewhere. We simply don't think to ask where that might be. In Scripture, the origin of the direction of our will is the desire of the heart. We are not ultimately able to direct our desires, since our desires are what give us all direction. The origin of our desires is our nature. Our nature is the core of who we are. Our nature is what defines our identity, and our identity is sinful due to the nature that Adam has passed down to us.

This leads to the most profound question that Scripture brings us to ask. If our nature is the root of our desires and Adam was created good, then how did Adam's good nature produce an evil desire? To say that his *free will* produced sin is to push the question of the origin of sin back into an eternal mystery. This would mean that Adam was able to produce evil desires independent of any aspect of his nature—therefore his sin came from nowhere in particular. This would leave us in a state of absolute randomness.

It is at this point that we must remain content with mystery. God cannot be charged with guilt for Adam's sin, yet we cannot articulate how one who was not made with sin produced sin. We also cannot say that Adam acted outside of what God planned to permit, and all that God permits, He permits for a reason. If indeed a creature could destroy the plans of God to this extent, then what should keep us from worrying that another fall might happen after God redeems the world?

There are times in which we must rest in the plans of God, knowing that He cannot fail. We must trust that even the worst tragedies will not violate God's eternal justice—no matter how much faith it requires of us. We should rest in the wise words of Martin Luther when he writes,

> But here God must be reverenced and held in awe, as being most merciful to those whom he justifies and saves in their own utter unworthiness; and we must show some measure of deference to His Divine wisdom by believing Him just when to us He seems unjust. If His justice were such as could be adjudged just by human reckoning, it clearly would not be Divine; it would in no way differ from human justice.[5]

[5]Martin Luther and John Dillenberger, *Martin Luther: Selections from His Writings* (New York: Anchor, 1958), 200.

The Layers of God's Desire

Why is it that God chooses to carry out His plan of salvation this way? Doesn't this scriptural truth imply that God has the power to save all people without violating their freedom? Are we reading the Scriptures right when they seem to say He has a desire to see all people come to salvation, or at least all kinds of people (1 Timothy 2:4)? Doesn't Scripture say that He doesn't delight in the destruction of evil people (Ezekiel 18:23)? If this is all true, then why does He not use this power? Why not save all? To answer this question, we must look further in Paul's words in Romans 9.

After expressing God's choice to have mercy on whom He wills, Paul continues,

> You will say to me then, Why does he still find fault? For who can resist his will? But who are you, O man, to answer back to God? Will what is molded say to its molder, why have you made me like this? Has the potter no right over the clay, to make out of the same lump one vessel for honorable use and another for dishonorable use? What if God, desiring to show his wrath and to make known his power, has endured with much patience vessels of wrath prepared for destruction, in order to make known the riches of his glory for vessels of mercy, which he has prepared beforehand for glory—even us whom he has called, not from the Jews only but also from the Gentiles? (Romans 9:19-24)

Perhaps the best way to answer such a difficult question is expressed right here—in the words of Paul. While God may indeed have it in His heart to see salvation come to pass, it is not the only desire in His heart. He is indeed a God of love, but that is not the only aspect of His nature. He is also a God of justice. He is a God who desires to let the power of His wrath be seen. This seems to be the central message of Romans 9. He wants the full value of His glory to be clearly perceived. He does it to make Himself known to those for whom He pours out mercy. He does it that we may be truly righteous by valuing Him for all that He is. Because there is no innate righteousness in humanity that draws God to any particular individual, God's choice of those for whom He will show mercy must be unconditional. This is what many Reformed theologians have called unconditional election.

While there are many passages that speak of God's love for the world, there is a much greater emphasis on God's particular love for His covenant people. While there are passages that may speak of an accomplishment of the cross that applies to the world, it is clear that it accomplished a very specific work for God's elect. It didn't simply purchase a universal offer of salvation, but it also purchased the heart-changing effects of the new covenant that Jesus referenced during the Last Supper (Jeremiah 31:31-34, Luke 22:30). While God calls all people to repentance with full foresight of their resistance, He purchases repentance for His elect. This could possibly be the distinction Paul is addressing when he writes to Timothy, "We have our hope set on the living God, who is the Savior of all people, *especially* of those who believe (1 Timothy 4:10, emphasis added). While God has great mercy on unbelievers in this life, He purchases the eternal salvation of those whom He has unconditionally chosen to bring to faith.

Perseverance

This leads us to the final portion of our passage in Romans 8. Paul makes it clear that God's calling leads to justification. If justification is by faith and justification is based on a calling originated in the eternal plan of God, then the call of God must contain the power to grant justifying faith. Theologians have often called this an *effectual* call. It contains what it requires.

In the final portion, Paul then says, "...those whom he justified he also glorified" (Romans 8:30). This raises one more penetrating question that we will explore. Why is it that Paul sees the end of our salvation, namely our glorification, as something that can be referred to in the past tense? Clearly, in the mind of Paul, glorification is a guarantee for those who have been justified. Paul sees salvation as a concept that is sealed in the mind of God. Is this true? Is it really impossible for someone to come to eternal destruction once he has been justified? This question has divided Christians throughout the history of the church.

While Paul seems confident in this passage, there are also passages in which he warns of eternal destruction, apparently to Christians. What is the reason for this? Is Paul contradicting himself? Even Jesus seemed to have confidence that He was able to keep those who were His when he said, "This is the will of him who sent me, that I should lose nothing of all that he has given me, but raise it up on the last day" (John 6:39).

What are we to do with this apparent tension? Could there be a unity in the mind of the biblical writers behind what seem to be irreconcilable ideas? What is it that Paul is doing in many of his letters as he exhorts his people to persevere in the faith?

While we are not sure of the author, the book of Hebrews has many of the characteristics of Paul's writings. Two of the most popular passages come from Hebrews which Christians use to support the possibility for us to lose our salvation (Chapters 6 and 10). While we will not look at these passages in great detail here, we will point out a text in an earlier chapter that may be of great help in sorting out how these two emphases go together. If God will most assuredly bring us to glorification, then why do biblical authors exhort us to persevere in the faith? In chapter 3, the author of Hebrews writes something very interesting:

> Exhort one another every day, as long as it is called today, that none of you may be hardened by the deceitfulness of sin. For we *have* come to share in Christ, *if* indeed we hold our original confidence firm to the end.
> (Hebrews 3:13-14, emphasis added)

What an odd way of encouraging one's readers. What the author does is take the holding of our confidence and makes it a fruit of our past and present reality of sharing in Christ. Rather than making this guaranteed result of sharing in Christ an excuse for laziness, the author makes it a reason for perseverance. This is the paradox of biblical perseverance. We are indeed to be confident that God will hold us firmly to the end, but this is not an excuse—it is a motivation. The guarantee of final salvation is a motivation for holy living in the heart that has been truly born again.

If indeed we could throw away so great a salvation and step out of the loving hands of God, then what is the real difference between the old covenant and the new? Israel failed to live up to the law of God over and over again. The purpose of the new covenant is to give the people a heart that would finally persevere (Ezekiel 36:27).

This is what the call of God is. It is a destiny that was decided before the foundations of the earth by which He saves us through His predestining grace and calls us with an effectual calling. He awakens our hearts that we would love Him and then progressively makes us more holy. While we should never blame God for the remnants of sin He allows to stay in us during this process, just as he has not yet destroyed the devil, we should never fear that our sin has taken us out of the hand of God. We should grieve and walk in repentance over what evil remains, and we should thank God for every step toward holiness, knowing that every weakness, every misstep, and every victory falls within His sovereign plan.

Recommended Reading

Edwards, Jonathan. *The Freedom of the Will,* Jonathan Edwards. London: Sovereign Grace Publishers, Inc., 2008.

Piper, John. *The Justification of God: an Exegetical and Theological Study of Romans 9:1-23.* Grand Rapids, Mich.: Baker Academic, 1993.

Sproul, R. C. *Chosen by God.* Grand Rapids, Mich.: Tyndale House Publishers, Inc., 1994.

Storms, Sam. *Chosen for Life: the Case for Divine Election.* Wheaton, Illinois: Crossway, 2007.

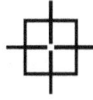

The Church

Christ loved the church and gave himself up for her, that he might sanctify her, having cleansed her by the washing of water with the word, so that he might present the church to himself in splendor, without spot or wrinkle or any such thing, that she might be holy and without blemish.

~Ephesians 5:25-27

The Commission

After Christ's resurrection and appearance to His followers, the time came for Him to go back to heaven. When His crucifixion was approaching, He had spoken of this moment. He had told His disciples what was to come, and He made them a promise. After finishing His teaching at the last supper, He said,

These things I have spoken to you while I am still with you. But the Helper, the Holy Spirit, whom the Father will send in my name, he will teach you all things and bring to your remembrance all that I have said to you.

(John 14:25-26)

It is in this passage that Jesus begins to reveal the way He will maintain the disciples' work of ministry after He has left them.

When the time finally comes for Him to depart, Matthew speaks of the final instructions that Jesus gave to them:

> Jesus came and said to them, All authority in heaven and on earth has been given to me. Go therefore and make disciples of all nations, baptizing them in the name of the Father and of the Son and of the Holy Spirit, teaching them to observe all that I have commanded you. And behold, I am with you always, to the end of the age.
>
> (Matthew 28:18-20)

There are many details in this passage on which we will focus, and some will take us into other areas of the New Testament.

In the passages we have examined, Jesus spoke of a number of things. He spoke of the giving of the Holy Spirit who would bring His teachings to remembrance, going into all nations and making disciples, and baptism. These are all incredibly central ideas in the lives of Christians today. How is it that we can see the way the disciples understood the words of Jesus in these passages?

The Day of Pentecost

In the book of Acts, the second work of Luke, we see some more instructions that Jesus left with His followers. Luke, while speaking of Jesus, says,

> While staying with them he ordered them not to depart from Jerusalem, but to wait for the promise of the Father, which, he said, "you heard from me; for John baptized with water, but you will be baptized with the Holy Spirit not many days from now."

> (Acts 1:4-5)

What we see is that while Jesus had certainly given a mission and a promise to the disciples, He also told them that they had to wait to be equipped for the promise before they began their mission.

In the following chapter, we can see the fulfillment of this promise. The Scriptures speak of it as the day of "Pentecost." It happened when the followers of Christ were all gathered in a room together. They were most likely praying and speaking of all they had learned during the life of Jesus. Luke then writes of an incredible event that took place,

> Suddenly there came from heaven a sound like a mighty rushing wind, and it filled the entire house where they were sitting. And divided tongues as of fire appeared to them and rested on each one of them. And they were all filled with the Holy Spirit and began to speak in other tongues as the Spirit gave them utterance.

> (Acts 2:2-4)

What the disciples were waiting for was not instruction from Jesus, but for power to fulfill what He had already commanded them to do. In this passage we see Him fill them with the Holy Spirit, just as He promised. We see the manifestation of signs. Those in the room began speaking in other tongues. Later in the passage we see that those who were there from other nations were able to understand the words being spoken (Acts 2:5-12).

The Birth of the Church

It is from this point that the message of Jesus began to spread. As people began to put their faith in Jesus, they began to gather together and learn more about who this Jesus was and what it meant to follow Him. After Peter shared a call to repentance following the coming of the Holy Spirit, Luke writes of the response:

> So those who received his word were baptized, and there were added that day about three thousand souls. And they devoted themselves to the apostles' teaching and the fellowship, to the breaking of bread and the prayers. And awe came upon every soul, and many wonders and signs were being done through the apostles. And all who believed were together and had all things in common. And they were selling their possessions and belongings and distributing the proceeds to all, as any had need. And day by day, attending the temple together and

breaking bread in their homes, they received their food with glad and generous hearts, praising God and having favor with all the people. And the Lord added to their number day by day those who were being saved.

(Acts 2:41-47)

There were clearly a great many things that came about as a result of the gospel message. It was this gospel message that began what is known today as "the Church." There are a few characteristics of these early Christians that we will examine. It is from their model that we gain a great deal of our church practices today, both from this passage and from others. We will focus on the Apostles' teaching, baptism, prayer, praising God, spiritual gifts, the breaking of bread, and good works.

The Apostles' Teaching

It is clear from texts like the ones we have just reviewed that the foundation for what Christians are to believe is built on what the Holy Spirit put in the mouths of the first Apostles. How is it that we are to apply this practice today when the original Apostles are long dead? The answer is very simple. Just as the Holy Spirit inspired the Apostles to preach the gospel and teach new disciples the words of Jesus, He inspired them to find ways of writing these teachings down. This is what the New Testament is.

A few centuries into the history of the Church, our fathers in the faith gathered into one Bible both the

Old Testament as well as the authoritative writings of the Apostles and those who learned directly from them—the New Testament. This made what we now know as the canon of scripture. Therefore, for us to devote ourselves to the Apostles' teaching today, we are to be a people that devotes itself to the Bible.

It is clear in the New Testament that as the Apostles were passing down their teaching, they encouraged that Scripture be the foundation of church instruction. We can even see this in Paul's encouragement of Timothy:

> From childhood you have been acquainted with the sacred writings, which are able to make you wise for salvation through faith in Christ Jesus. All Scripture is breathed out by God and profitable for teaching, for reproof, for correction, and training in righteousness, that the man of God may be competent, equipped for every good work.
>
> (2 Timothy 3:15-16)

While it is most likely that Paul was speaking of the Old Testament in this passage, it is clear from other authors that the writings of the Apostles were also gaining authority and were also beginning to be considered Scripture. It was Peter himself who referred to Paul's writings as being on par with the Old Testament (2 Peter 3:16).

Baptism

As people came to faith in Christ, they would couple their confession of Jesus Christ as Lord with the act of Baptism. This was meant to symbolize the supernatural connection we have with Christ as we put our faith in Him. As Paul says in Romans, "We were buried therefore with him by baptism into death, in order that, just as Christ was raised from the dead by the glory of the Father, we too might walk in newness of life" (Romans 6:4).

Throughout church history there has been great misunderstanding surrounding baptism. Very early in church history, church leaders began to see baptism as a direct parallel with the Old Testament symbol of circumcision. They did this even though it is a symbol of faith and therefore should be applied to those who are old enough to express the gift of faith. Therefore it began to be applied to the children of those who were in the church. This may not have been an unreasonable conclusion, since circumcision was also a symbol of faith but was still applied to infants in the Old Testament (Romans 4:11, Leviticus 12:3).

However, what this understanding assumed was more similarity between the old and new covenants than actually existed. In the Old Covenant, being born into a Jewish family automatically meant entrance into the people of God. However, Paul states clearly that the people of God today are not gathered in this way. He states, "It is not the children of the flesh who are the children of God, but the children of the promise are counted as offspring" (Romans 9:8). This refers yet again to to Paul's teaching on election. Since our salvation is not based on our lineage, we are to baptize people not directly after their birth in the flesh, but after their birth in the Spirit—what Jesus called being "born again" (John 3).

Once people put their faith in Christ, they are to make a public declaration of this event by being immersed in water before the people of God. This symbolizes their new life in Christ and the fact that they have given everything to Him.

Prayer

From the start of the church, even from the instructions of the Lord Jesus Himself, the practice of prayer has been kept by God's people. Prayer quite simply is speaking and communing either individually or corporately with God. Because Christ has made a way to approach the Father through His blood, we can now pray to the Father in the name of Jesus Christ by the power of the Holy Spirit.

Prayer can include anything from repentance, to giving thanks, to making our needs and requests known to God. While God does have a plan that was set in motion before the foundations of the earth, He has included our prayers as a means by which He will carry out those plans. Because of this we can pray simply and confidently that God is able to do anything we ask so long as it is done out of a desire to live according to His will. Prayer not only can change what happens around us, but it can change us more into the image of God as we remain in His presence.

Praising God

Another way in which we may express our worship in a public gathering, besides hearing from Scripture, prayer, and baptizing new disciples, is to sing songs to God. This is often done with all kinds of instruments. We may sing songs from throughout our history or perhaps something new that someone among us has written. Paul sums up this practice by saying,

> Be filled with the Holy Spirit, addressing one another in psalms and hymns and spiritual songs, singing and making melody to the Lord with your heart, giving thanks always and for everything to God the Father and the Lord Jesus Christ.
>
> (Ephesians 5:18-20)

Spiritual Gifts

Another great reality which can be found in the New Testament is that there were supernatural manifestations that took place in the life of the local church. In his writings, Paul calls these spiritual gifts. This is when God gives Himself to His people by the power of His Holy Spirit.

There are certain gifts that guide in the governing of the church, such as teaching and pastoring. These are briefly listed among the spiritual gifts and Paul also outlines the qualifications for oversight and eldership positions in his pastoral letters (1 Timothy, Titus).

There are also many gifts that manifest in the everyday life of the church body. Some examples would be such things as prophecy, when God gives a future insight or word of exhortation. There can be such things as supernatural knowledge given to Christians by which they can apply biblical truth in ways they could never do without God's supernatural help. Another is speaking in spiritual tongues by which we can edify our spirit. There are times when we can ask God for supernatural healings and He answers. While Paul says that we should desire spiritual gifts, he also makes it clear that God gives these gifts as He pleases. Not every gift is given to every person, but God distributes them as he sees fit. These gifts and several others are described by Paul and are outlined in greater detail in 1 Corinthians 12-14 with guidelines concerning how they should be exercised.

Communion

Another practice that can be seen in the New Testament is the church "breaking bread" together. There are two things this may refer to. At times it may refer to the sharing of meals in each others' homes. This may be done today as Christians gather to discuss the word of God and meet each other's spiritual needs. It many at times also be referring to what is known as the sacrament of communion.

At the last supper, Jesus presented His disciples with a way in which He wanted them to remember Him. He gave them wine and bread and told them to divide them amongst themselves. He told them that these were His body and blood which were poured out for them, and brought about the new covenant. He told them to remember Him as often as they divided these elements amongst themselves (Luke 22:17-20).

Unfortunately this sacrament has also been misunderstood throughout church history. Many Christians have taken this teaching to mean that the bread and wine truly turn into the sacrificial body and blood of Christ. However, this understanding doesn't take into account the fact that Christ called this an act of "remembrance." It seems quite clear that this was simply to be a symbol by which we put our faith in the sacrifice of Christ which was given once for *all* time (Hebrews 9:26). It is an opportunity for Christians to corporately exercise their faith in the great work that Christ did on the cross.

Good Works

One last thing we will point out in the Scripture is the incredible love that the early church had for each other as well as for the rest of the world. Luke makes it abundantly clear that they were eager to meet each other's needs. They shared their belongings. They opened their homes to one another. They were in good standing with the community that surrounded them.

What many fear when they hear the gospel of free grace, by which we are saved through faith and not works, is that there will no longer be a motivation to do good works.

However, it is clear that the New Testament writers saw no tension between these two realities.

In the book of Ephesians, Paul places good works exactly where they should belong in the mind of the Christian when he says,

> For by grace you have been saved through faith. And this is not your own doing; it is the gift of God, not a result of works, so that no one may boast. For we are his workmanship, created in Christ Jesus for good works, which God prepared beforehand, that we should walk in them.
>
> (Ephesians 2:8-10)

We are not saved by our good works. We are never again to do them out of fear. We are to do them out of thanks and out of love because God has given us salvation and has put us into a Christian body of believers. This not only applies to the church body we find ourselves in, but we should be inspired to live with a love for the world outside of the church, loving without condition and always inviting others to join into a life lived in the gospel.

We also continue in the great commission which was given to us by Jesus. We continue to go into the world and preach the gospel to every nation as we are made able. Our invitation into the life of the gospel is never meant to remain local but is to reach out to all that have need in every corner of the world, just as the original Apostles began to do in their surrounding nations.

These are some of the many characteristics of the local church as well as the universal church which contains every believer that has ever lived. It is a life of worship lived in loving response to the grace that God has extended to His people. The church is meant to be a body of people that bleeds with love for her community and her world in a way that manifests itself in a practical as well as a verbal declaration of the gospel.

Recommended Reading

DeYoung, Kevin, and Greg Gilbert. *What Is the Mission of the Church?* Wheaton Illinois: Crossway, 2011.

DeYoung, Kevin, and Ted Kluck. *Why We Love the Church.* Chicago, Illinois: Moody, 2009.

Storms, Sam. *The Beginner's Guide to Spiritual Gifts.* Ventura, California: Regal, 2004.

Storms, Sam. *Convergence: Spiritual Journeys of a Charismatic Calvinist.* 1st Edition ed. Edmond, OK: Enjoying God Ministries, 2005.

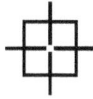

The End

For now we see in a mirror dimly, but then face to face. Now I know in part; then I shall know fully, even as I have been fully known.
~ 1 Corinthians 13:12

The Kingdom of God

When Jesus first came to earth and began to beckon people to come to repentance, He was preaching to a people that was expecting a great Messiah. Not only were they expecting someone to come to teach them, they were expecting a great king to come and conquer the earth with his rule. They expected that God would establish an eternal kingdom on the earth. This explains why there was such disappointment when Jesus was killed. Everyone expected Him to establish what His people had been waiting to see for hundreds of years. In the gospels of Matthew and Mark, we see the disciples ask Jesus about the establishment of the kingdom of God. He answers in a very strange way.

He doesn't say that He is about to establish the kingdom. He has already spoken to His disciples about the fact that he must leave. He speaks of the destruction of the temple in Jerusalem and the fact that there would be war and persecution after He has left. The question then is not whether or not He is on the verge of establishing the kingdom, but are these wars and persecutions signs of a *second* coming of Christ? The kingdom was not to be eternally established in His first coming. What is His answer concerning the time of his second coming? These signs are not signs of His return, but are only birth pangs. No one actually knows when He will return (Matthew 24, Mark 13).

Three Perspectives

There was only one remaining Apostle who was not killed as a result of preaching of the gospel, and that was John. Toward the end of his life, he wrote a letter to seven churches that were under his care while on the prison island of Patmos. This letter is now called "Revelation." The letter was the summary of what he had seen when Jesus Christ appeared to him there. He gives warnings as well as encouragement to each of those churches according to the words that Jesus Christ spoke.

After he did this, however, he began to write with a great amount of symbolism. These writings have led to more diverse interpretation throughout church history than any other book in the New Testament. Book upon book has been written about the book of Revelation. We will look at three different perspectives on one portion of that book. The portion we will examine is Chapter 20:1-6. Rather than quote the passage at length here, I recommend that you follow along with an open Bible as you read this chapter. That way you can interpret the passage for yourself and see it in its surrounding context. It is here that we see the end of the world as we know it. We see Christ ruling for a millennium and then destroying all evil. This is then followed by the establishment of a new heaven and a new earth that lasts for eternity. While many people differ over details throughout Revelation, this is where the greatest differences in understanding become clear.

Premillenialism

The three perspectives we will mention are divided by their views of our relationship to the Millennium which is described in Revelation 20:1-6. They differ in how they describe the point at which Christ will return in relation to that time period. Throughout church history, Premillenialism is a perspective that has stood for a long time and can be seen in the writings of many church fathers. This perspective sees the time where we stand in history as standing *before* the Millennial reign of Christ. Premillenialists believe that Revelation should be read as a linear story and therefore the Millennium lies at the end of history. We have yet to experience it.

For many who hold to this understanding, a time of great persecution is believed to come toward the end of the age and will culminate when Christ returns, but this will not be the final state. He will bind the devil for the duration of the millennium so he will no longer be able to deceive the nations. The devil will then be released for a short time leading up to his final destruction and the destruction of his followers. After this is finished and all the enemies of Christ are destroyed, Christ will set up the eternal state and Christians will reign forever with Him on the earth.

Under the heading of Premillenialism, there is a more specific understanding of this issue, called Dispensational Premillenialism. In this perspective, there are a few other events that are believed to surround the coming of Christ's millennial reign, and they come from different interpretations of many Old Testament passages which we will not cover in detail here.

According to this view, there will indeed be a great tribulation at the end of church history, but somewhere in the midst of this tribulation there will be a sudden rapture of the church. We will suddenly be caught up into heaven and we will remain with Christ until the tribulation is over. It is believed that the tribulation will last for seven years. Premillenialists differ concerning whether the rapture will happen before, during, or after this tribulation takes place. When it is over, the millennial reign of Christ will begin and history will finish just as classic historical Premillenialism understands it. This view came into being during the 1800s and was popularized by the popular "Left Behind" book series.

Amillennialism

To understand this view, we need to take on a very different perspective concerning the way Revelation is meant to be read. According to this view, the book of Revelation should be read as seven parallel accounts of Christ's reign over church history. This matches with the fact that Revelation is addressed to seven churches. With this perspective in place, Revelation 20:1-6 and the millennial reign of Christ take on a very different meaning.

Rather than being a future millennial reign of Christ, it is regarded as a symbol of Christ's heavenly reign that began at the destruction of the temple of Jerusalem in 70 AD. It is believed that the great persecution surrounding this event is what Revelation is referring to when it speaks of the great tribulation. While many Amillennialists may view the great tribulation as a pattern that Christians can expect to continue until today, some believe in a future tribulation of great magnitude as well. Still, the basic meaning of the tribulation is seen as this past event surrounding the destruction of the temple.

With this understanding in place, Amillennialists are then able to view the coming of Christ as a singular event which will bring about the destruction of evil and the establishment of the eternal state in the new heavens and the new earth. In this perspective, there remains an understanding of continuing persecution as well as the permanent need to spread the gospel. Amillennialism is a perspective which can be held without focusing so much on the idea of Christ's return being accompanied by various signs that we need to interpret. His return is seen as inevitable, but beyond our ability to predict.

Postmillennialism

In many ways, this perspective is similar to Amillennialism in that the millennial reign of Christ is seen as a present reality. The difference comes when you ask where the millennial reign of Christ is taking place. Rather than being a heavenly reign which leaves the earth in a presently decaying state until Christ returns, Christ's millennial reign, though spiritual, is an earthly reign.

According to this perspective, Christians are not merely working for the spread of the gospel in the midst of persecution, they believe they are bringing about a Christianized world in which sin is being defeated and eventually will be an exception rather than a rule. After the world is converted to Christ, it is believed that He will finally return and establish the eternal state.

Different Emphases

Within these three main views, there are dangers as well as benefits. That is not to say that they are all correct or that we cannot work to discover which is most faithful to Scripture, but in the midst of disagreement we should understand the strengths of each position as well as possible dangers if different points within each of them are focused on too much.

In Premillenialism as well as Amillennialism, there tends to be a very strong emphasis on gospel proclamation. This is obviously a good thing. These two positions maintain a ballast by which they maintain the purity of the gospel in the midst of whatever persecution tends to come their way. On the other hand, these two perspectives may lead to a premature pessimism concerning the world we live in. While persecution is a reality, this doesn't mean that we are merely waiting to escape from the earth and that we should hide whenever we aren't preaching the gospel. There is a place for social justice efforts to make the world a better place in whatever ways we can while we wait for the Lord to return.

In Postmillennialism, the focus is often reversed. Because the goal is to make the world operate according to Christian principles, persecution is not necessarily seen as a reality that will remain until Christ returns. Social justice and worldwide respect for the Christian mindset is often made the goal. This at times may lead to a lack of emphasis on the pure and basic preaching of the gospel. Since tangible results are expected to be seen in society, a lack of progress at any given time may lead to a doubt that the gospel is being preached properly. This may lead to an underestimation of the sinfulness of the human heart and a surprised attitude in response to great resistance. This has a danger of causing Christians to sand away the rough edges of Christianity.

On the other hand, Christians who hold to this mindset are more likely to bring the church into better standing with the world around them. They are more likely to have an optimistic outlook on the future of righteousness in the world and therefore will likely maintain a passionate heart for justice.

Finding Unity

One thing must be stated before we close this chapter. As diverse as our understanding may be in the church concerning the nature of the way the world as we know it will end, we agree on some very foundational truths. Christ came. Christ died. Christ rose. Christ is coming again. These truths are held by all who believe in orthodox Christianity, and these truths must be maintained in the midst of whatever disagreement we have.

As Christians from all three of these ways of thinking interact with each other, there are a few things that must never divide us. First, the gospel is absolutely central. No matter what success or failure we have in spreading it, we should not question whether its foundational doctrines ought to be shared. We should never compromise our gospel core.

Second, Christians should be passionate about social justice. This isn't because our social concerns will justify us; but because we are at peace with God, we should be passionate about spreading the good news about the relationship we now have with Him. Social change should be the means for and the result of the embrace of the gospel.

If we keep these truths central, we shouldn't have anything to fear. While we should certainly work hard to see what the scripture means concerning these issues, we should not divide over them. We should press on into the future and be ready to preach the gospel in whatever circumstance we face. Jesus promised that He would be with us.

Recommended Reading

Boettner, Loraine, Anthony Hoekema, Herman Hoyt, and George Ladd. *The Meaning of the Millennium: Four Views*. Edited by Robert Clouse. Downers Grove, Illinois: InterVarsity Press, 1996.

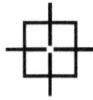

Summary

What has hopefully just been given to you is a basic but thorough outline of the doctrines of the Christian faith. Our faith is most certainly not a simplistic thing, nor should it be. It addresses a world that has been made by God and beckons us to submit every area of our life to His eternal rule. We are creatures made in the image of God. We have rebelled against Him. Yet thanks be to Him that He didn't leave us in our hopeless condition.

Before the foundations of the earth, God had a purpose to express His glory in the most profound form possible—His grace. He sent His Son into the world to teach us the true nature of the Father as it was revealed in the Old Testament. He lived a perfect life. He died a terrible death. He took the wrath of the Father upon Himself. He was then buried. Three days later He rose again by the power of God.

We now have hope that if we put our faith in Him, we can be saved from all our rebellion. Not only are we forgiven, but we are given the very righteousness of our Savior. As we contemplate the plan of God, we know that "For our sake he made him to be sin who knew no sin, so that in him we might become the righteousness of God" (2 Corinthians 5:21).

Now that we have been justified in the sight of God, we are able to walk in righteousness by the power of the Holy Spirit. We can walk in hope that even when we die, we will be in the presence of God. Not only that, but one day we will receive new bodies and will rule with Christ in the new heavens and the new earth.

Until then, we are at home among the people of God. God has made a way for us to fellowship with one another. We are able to come together in worship and we can hear from God's Word and sing praises to His name. We are able to live all of life together, beckoning the world to experience the power of the gospel. We can now walk in love, knowing that God is working out His sovereign plan in our lives until the day Christ finally returns.

God bless you as you live the Christian life.

Eric J.

www.ingramcontent.com/pod-product-compliance
Lightning Source LLC
Chambersburg PA
CBHW072019060426
42446CB00044B/2942